Exercise and Health

American Academy
of Physical Education Papers
No. 17

EXERCISE AND HEALTH

American Academy
of Physical Education Papers
No. 17

Fifty-fourth Annual Meeting
Minneapolis, Minnesota
April 6-7, 1983

Published by Human Kinetics Publishers, Inc.
for the American Academy of Physical Education

EDITORS
Helen M. Eckert
Henry J. Montoye

Academy Seal designed by
R. Tait McKenzie

ISBN 0-931250-56-0
ISSN 0741-4633

Printed in the United States of America

Copies of this publication may be ordered from:

Human Kinetics Publishers, Inc.
Box 5076, Champaign, IL 61820
(217) 351-5076

Contents

INTRODUCTION
Henry J. Montoye   1

EXERCISE AND HEALTH: LESSONS FROM THE PAST
Allan J. Ryan   3

EXERCISE AND RISK OF CORONARY HEART DISEASE
Arthur S. Leon   14

EXERCISE AND RESTING BLOOD PRESSURE
Charles M. Tipton   32

RECENT PROGRESS IN UNDERSTANDING OBESITY
Lawrence B. Oscai   42

EXERCISE AND ARTHROPATHY
Bruno Balke   49

EXERCISE AND OSTEOPOROSIS
Henry J. Montoye   59

EXERCISE AND THE PHYSIOLOGY OF AGING
Herbert A. deVries   76

EXERCISE AS A FACTOR
IN AGING MOTOR BEHAVIOR PLASTICITY
Waneen Wyrick Spirduso   89

THE LONGEVITY, MORBIDITY, AND PHYSICAL FITNESS OF FORMER ATHLETES—AN UPDATE
K.E. Stephens, W.D. Van Huss, H.W. Olson, and H.J. Montoye   101

ATHLETIC AMENORRHEA: A REVIEW
Barbara L. Drinkwater   120

PHYSICAL ACTIVITY AND MENTAL HEALTH
William P. Morgan   132

PRESIDENT'S ADDRESS—THE FUTURE AGENDA
Edward J. Shea   146

PRESIDENTS, THE AMERICAN ACADEMY OF PHYSICAL EDUCATION   153

Introduction

Henry J. Montoye
University of Wisconsin-Madison

A study of the history of education in the United States will reveal that at one time health was the focus of physical education. In time the emphasis shifted, but in recent years the pendulum has swung back again. This is not difficult to understand. At the turn of the century our health problems were different from those of today. Gradually certain infectious and childhood diseases came under control, and now we are left mostly with traffic accidents (particularly in the young) and the chronic diseases and disabilities of middle and old age. The latter are intimately associated with our living habits, including exercise habits.

In our industrialized society, advanced technology makes it difficult, even for blue-collar workers, to exercise regularly. Today's modes of transportation have further reduced our opportunities for physical activity. These two factors—the increasing significance of chronic diseases and the decreasing opportunities for exercise—have led to increased medical problems associated with a sedentary life.

Clearly, prevention is the answer to our present day health problems. Even the best cardiac rehabilitation programs, for example, will be of little use to many heart attack victims—almost half of them don't survive the first 24 hours. Furthermore, it is much more expensive to arrest or cure disease than to prevent it.

The chronic diseases and disabilities that plague our middle-aged and older Americans generally begin early in life. Hence prevention, if it is to be effective, must begin in young people. Furthermore, although a sedentary life is responsible for some of our ill health, who is in the best position to do something about it? Certainly not the physician, who frequently is overwhelmed with diagnosis and treatment. And there is no sign that the physician will have more time for educational aspects of preventive medicine among children and young adults. Besides, the physician and his or her staff deal mostly with the sick, not the young and healthy in whom prevention must be practiced. Clearly, then, it is the health and physical educator who must play a vital role here.

Because of these developments, there is now more motivation and opportunity to investigate the relationship of exercise to health than at any other time in history. Hence, research findings related to the theme of this year's meeting are being published at an accelerating rate. It is becoming impossible to stay abreast of developments in this broad field. Consequently, it is important for experts to bring us up to date on a topic that serves as a foundation of the physical education profession. In addition, the theme has implications for one's personal health and well-being.

Exercise and Health:
Lessons From the Past

Allan J. Ryan
Editor-in-Chief, The Physician and Sportsmedicine

The concept of health is so ancient that it precedes any knowledge of the true nature and causes of disease. It has generally been considered in relation to the ability of the individual to function independently and adequately in society to satisfy personal needs for food, shelter, employment, care of family members, and recreation. Even in times when illness, diseases, and death were related to constitutional characteristics, mental attitudes, and perhaps divine intervention, there were philosophers who attempted to define perfect health as a complete absence of any bodily sickness or deformity.

Galen, a Greco-Roman physician of the 2nd century, was very impatient with this point of view. In his writings on hygiene (de Sanitate Tuenda) he said:

> But if anyone shall say that only those are healthy who function perfectly in all their parts, and that we others who function less well are not healthy, let him know that he is undermining the entire consideration of hygiene. For if the object of this consideration is to preserve the health we received from the beginning, but no one of us is healthy, it is clear that the art of hygiene is useless and futile. . . . that which is indivisible and which at the same time is, and is called health, is not merely absolute in itself, but that which falls short of this is not nevertheless unsuitable for our purposes. For we all need health, not only for the functions of life which diseases impede, interrupt or destroy, but also that we may avoid disease. For we are afflicted no little with pain; but that condition in which we do not suffer pain, and are not impeded in the activities of life, we call health" (Galen, trans. by Green, 1951)

This functional concept of health did not originate with Galen, but it had probably never been better expressed and, since it was preserved in his writings which dominated medical thinking for hundreds of years afterward, had an extraordinary and lasting influence. The written tradition relating physical activity and both active and passive exercise to the preservation and restoration of health can be traced back at least to the Ayur-Veda (Guthrie, 1945) in the 9th century B.C., in which exercise and massage are recommended for the treatment of rheumatism. Herodicus, the Greek gymnast (one of three classes of medical practitioners), in the 5th century B.C. based his therapeutics chiefly on vigorous exercise (LeClerc, 1723) and was criticized for so doing by his contemporary, Hippocrates. This man, whom we honor as the father of medicine, referred often in his own works (Littre, 1839-1861) to the values of exercise, however, prescribing it even for mental illness.

In the absence of specific therapeutics, it is not surprising that physicians would recommend exercise since they could easily recognize the vigor and vitality of those who performed vigorous exercise either as athletes or soldiers; and it also had the magical element of imitating the behavior that was desired, the restoration of normal physical activity. Herophilus and Eristratus at Alexandria in the 4th century B.C. recommended moderate exercise (Adams, 1844), and Asclepiades in the 1st century B.C. recommended walking and running for his patients (Asclepiades, trans. 1955). Aristotle, the teacher of the young men in the court of Philip of Macedon and tutor of Alexander the Great, agreed with these ideas when he said, "The following are examples of the results of action: bodily health is the result of a fondness for gymnastics; a man falls into ill health as a result of not caring for exercise" (Ross, 1928-1952).

Although we think of Greek learning as being lost during the Middle Ages and rediscovered during the Renaissance, the medical knowledge and traditions were preserved through the Arabs and perpetuated through the medical school at Salerno from the 10th to 13th centuries. In the great poem of medicine, the Regimen Sanitatis Salernitamun, coming from that school in the 12th century, exercise is mentioned twice as being therapeutic, as in "use exercise that vapours ill consumes" (Joseph, 1949). Moses Maimonides, the Jewish philosopher-physician of the 12th century, wrote, "Anyone who lives a sedentary life and does not exercise. . . . even if he eats good foods and takes care of himself according to proper medical principles — all his days will be painful ones and his strength shall wane" (Maimonides, 1199).

For the young men of the medieval court, physical education began at the age of 14 with vigorous sports and exercises, including dancing and horsemanship, which is the basis of modern gymnastics. A boy had to be able to mount a horse quickly without stirrups and dismount from a running horse. Under old Saxon law this ability was proof of his being able to govern independently. In the Mirror of Knights it was specified that among other things he should be able to swim and dive, climb on ropes, jump, wrestle, and fence (Joseph, 1949).

With the advent of the Renaissance, scholars in Italy revived the interest in classic gymnastics and recommended it as a necessary part of the educational process. Petrarca (1304-1374), in his pamphlet "Against a Certain Physician" (Petrarca, 1354), recommended substituting exercise as a natural remedy as opposed to medicines which poison the body. Vittorino daFeltre took this much further and changed the spirit and direction of education completely, creating an influence that is still present today. Trained as a physician and accomplished as a classical scholar, daFeltre was called to the court of the Duke of Mantua to educate the young princes. He organized a school comparable to the English public school or the American country day school, where the student entered at age 4 or 5 and remained until his education was complete (McCormick, 1943-1944). Physical education preceded intellectual training at first and then accompanied it constantly.

Eventually children from the working classes were accepted, and each student was prescribed a type of exercise suited for his age, body, the season, and the time of day. Exercises included riding, fencing, dancing, swimming, wrestling, running, jumping, ball games, throwing the discus, hunting, fishing, and mock battles, all performed outdoors in both summer and winter. He felt that by exercise and diet he could change body constitution and at the same time develop the mind and the human spirit.

All humanistic educators of this period were in general accord regarding the importance of exercise to health as well as to education. Francesco Barbaro (1395-1440) wrote a book for his patron Lorenzo de Medici entitled *Prudent and Important Documents for the Choice of a Wife* (Barbaro, 1548) in which he recommended physical exercise for young women not only for their own health but also so that they might have healthy children. Leon Battista Alberti (1404-1472) in his educational work *Of the Family* (Joseph, 1949) recommends physical exercise beginning in early infancy as of the greatest importance in strengthening the muscles, stimulating the circulation, and adapting the nervous system. He pointed out that this became even more important with increasing age. Matteo Palmieri (1406-1475) recommended in his book (Palmieri, 1894) strenuous exercises including climbing mountains. Maffeus Vegius (1407-1458) in his *Education of Children and Their Good Habits* (Vegius, 1613) distinguished light recreational exercises from those heavy military ones designed to strengthen the body, and advised moderation in all actions. Juan Luis Vives (1492-1540) in the fourth book of his *On Instruction and on Christian Education* said exercise was indispensable to young students in refreshing and stimulating them to use intellectual as well as physical power (Vives, 1536).

Although the great educators of the 15th century had confirmed exercise as an important part of the educational process and recommended it as a lifelong habit, the physicians of the age had not taken it up with the same enthusiasm. The intellectual ferment in the 16th century, which was stimulated by the more general use of printing, affected medicine and began the great period of medical gymnastics. The leader in this activity, and a man whose influence became for the next 200 years as important as Galen's had been in previous centuries, was Hieronymus Mercurialis (1530-1606). His *Six Books on the Art of Gymnastics* (Mercuriale, 1569) established the principles and practice that have been followed in one form or another since then and have become the basis for what we know now as rehabilitation medicine. He wrote not only for physicians but also "for all persons interested in health" and quoted widely from poets, philosophers, and theologians, which emphasized the importance of what he had to say.

Every exercise he described was only from the standpoint of its usefulness to attaining and maintaining a state of health. He discarded passive exercises, which had been favored by many of his predecessors, and recommended only vigorous exercise involving strenuous breathing and great physical effort. He classified exercises as preventive and therapeutic, modifying their severity for the sick, but recommending that they be carried out in the open air in areas protected from the wind. Each exercise should preserve the existing healthy state, should not disturb the harmony between the principal humours, and should be suited to particular parts of the body. Convalescents and weakened older persons should have special exercises based on specific diagnoses which should not exacerbate their infirmities. All persons who lead sedentary lives, and he included scientists and prisoners in that number, need exercise urgently, he said.

He described three sorts of walking, including mountain climbing, and recommended running as a healthy exercise, jumping, rope climbing, wrestling, and ball games to strengthen the upper body. His follower Tuccaro (born ca 1535) published *Three Dialogues on the Acrobatics of Jumping* (Tuccaro, 1589) in which he described 53 varieties and said, "This robust and strong exercise has a tendency to expel excrements and to calm all sorts of humours." Ambroise Pare (1510-1590), the most famous surgeon of his day, in his *Surgery* (Pare, 1582) restated Galen's belief that the body needs exercise for health. He included breathing exercises, running, riding, carrying heavy loads, and massage, and considered exercises of the limbs following fractures to be essential to complete recovery. Joseph Duchesne (born 1544) wrote in his *Ars Medica Hermetica* (1648), "The essential purpose of gymnastics for the body is its deliverance from superfluous humours, the regulation of digestion, the strengthening of the heart and joints, the opening of the pores of the skin, and the stronger circulation of blood in the lungs by strenuous breathing." Swimming is recommended for the first time as a healthful exercise in this book. Laurent Joubert (1529-1583), professor of medicine at Montpellier, considered physicians as the only ones capable of prescribing gymnastics correctly (Joubert, 1582) and attached great importance to daily exercise.

In England during the 16th century, attitudes toward exercise were represented by the set of rules drawn up by James I (1567-1612) for the prince of Wales. He barred from his court "all rough and violent exercises" but recommended running, leaping, fencing, tennis, archery, and hunting with hounds (Joseph, 1949). The 17th century saw a growing interest in mechanics; publications dealing with human and animal involvement by writers such as Aldobrandinus (1616), Acquapendente (1614), Deusing (1656), and Perrault (1680) brought about great progress in muscle physiology. The stage was set for Francis Fuller to write,

> As for the exercise of the body, if people would not think so superficially of it, if they would but abstract the benefit got by it from the means by which it is got, they would set a great value upon it; if some of the advantages accruing from exercise were to be procured by any one medicine, nothing in the world would be in more esteem than that medicine would be; but as those advantages are to be obtained another way, and by taking some pains, men's heads are turned to overlook and slight them. (Fuller, 1704)

The essayist Joseph Addison (1672-1719) echoed these thoughts, saying, "Exercise ferments the humours, casts them into their proper channels, throws off tendencies and helps nature in their secret distributions without which the body cannot subsist in its vigor nor the soul act with cheerfulness." Platner in Germany bitterly expressed the opinion that people in his day failed to appreciate the importance of daily exercise to preserve a healthy body (Platner, 1734).

Joseph Tissot (1756-1826), a French military surgeon, in his *Medical and Surgical Gymnastics* (Tissot, 1780) recommended moderate exercise both for the healthy and for those recuperating from acute illness or suffering from a chronic disease. Nenci, professor of medicine at Siena, in 1766 published his *Discussion on Gymnastics With Regard to its Use in Medical Practice* (Nenci, 1766). An adherent to the medical-mathematical doctrine, he believed that movement was the source of life and that health depended on continuous equilibrated movement of fluids through innumerable channels in the body. Perspiration, on one hand, and a correct distribution of body fluids including blood, whose movement is stimulated by muscle contractions, on the other hand, would enhance the production of health-giving new humours. He suggested light daily exercises, long walks, and riding for healthy as well as drastically ill persons.

Nicolas Andry (1658-1742), professor of medicine at the Royal College of Paris, began a new approach in his *l'Orthopedie* (Andry,

1741), which created a new specialty called orthopedics. He began his book with these words: "No man lives to himself alone; we must avoid having an unpleasing appearance. Even if we were alone in the world, it is not permissible to neglect the body and deform it; it would be against the Creator's will." He advised parents to pay attention to the bodily development of their children from the time of infancy. He described not only exercises but also the proper construction of children's furniture to prevent deformed postures. He recommended daily exercises, substituting rural labor for gymnastics as necessary.

The Napoleonic wars at the beginning of the 19th century were primarily responsible for the development of a profession of physical education separate from medicine. Ling in Sweden (Westerblad, 1909) introduced systems into exercise, advising semiactive and semipassive resistance exercises. George Taylor (Taylor, 1860) introduced the system into America where it became very popular. Nachtegall in Copenhagen (Hackensmith, 1966), Clias in Berne (Clias, 1819), Jahn in Prussia (Hackensmith, 1966), and Amoros in Paris (Hackensmith, 1966) all contributed to the development of a true physical education and related its importance to health. Easton in England had published a book in 1799 about human longevity, in which he reported that he had studied 1,712 people over 100 years of age. He concluded, "It is not the rich nor the great, not those who depend on medicine, who became old, but such as use much exercise."

Already in the United States the great Philadelphia physician Benjamin Rush had in 1772 delivered a "Sermon on Exercise" (Runes, 1947) in which he recommended many types of sports and exercises including dancing for the old as well as the young. His *Plan of a Federal University* included exercises to improve the body's strength and elegance, as well as health. References to the values of exercise appeared regularly in American medical writing in the early 19th century. William P. Dewees published his *Treatise on the Physical and Medical Treatment of Children* (Dewees, 1826), in which he stated that exercise for both sexes developed good tone and vigor for all parts of the body. Dr. John Collins Watten published an essay on "The Importance of Physical Education," expanded to a book in 1845, entitled *Physical Education and the Preservation of Health*. Watten, with a group of other physicians and laymen, opened the Boston Gymnasium in 1825. John Eberle wrote, "The development of the moral and physical energies of children can in no way be more effectually promoted than by permitting them to engage freely in the usual sports of childhood in the fresh and open air" (Eberle, 1833).

No one stirred up more interest and excitement about exercise and physical fitness among the general public than the eclectic physician Sylvester Graham, the son and grandson of physicians. Beginning in

Philadelphia in 1830, he quickly became a national figure by lecturing and writing, developing Graham flour, bread, and crackers and establishing Graham boarding houses where people followed a prescribed diet and exercised regularly (Shryock, 1931).

School and popular texts on physiology multiplied rapidly and were read eagerly. Bell (1842) in his book *On Regimen and Longevity* noted the longevity of farmers who worked hard in the open air, and said that youthful activity determined future health and life but that development of great strength did not favor longevity.

In the years from the Civil War to World War I, the names of the physicians stand out as contributors to the knowledge and practice of how exercise helps promote and maintain good health: Edward Hitchcock, Dudley A. Sargent, William G. Anderson, R. Tait McKenzie. Their influence upon the public at large, as well as in the medicine and physical education professions, has been enormous. It provided the basis for our general acceptance of the relationship between exercise and a more rewarding and healthier life, our knowledge now amplified as to the particulars by great advances in what can be called the science of exercise, as well as in medicine.

Edward Hitchcock, Jr. (1828-1911), son of the third president of Amherst College, graduated from there in 1849 and from Harvard Medical School in 1853. He and his father published a work describing the relationship between exercise and health for boys and girls and said that gymnastics were as important to schools and colleges as libraries were (Hitchcock & Hitchcock, 1860). The next president, Stearns, concerned about the number of students dropping out of college because of poor health and two who died during the first 6 years of his administration, established a department of physical education and hygiene in 1859. The catalogue of 1861-62 stated,

> Its design is to secure healthful daily exercise and recreation to all students; to instruct them in the use of the vocal organs, movements of the body and manners as connected with oratory; and to teach them, both theoretically and practically, the laws of health. This daily physical training is a part of the regular college course. (Hitchcock, 1879)

Dr. Hitchcock was appointed the director of this department in 1861 and maintained the position for 50 years.

Dr. Hitchcock generally oversaw the health of all the students, lectured to them on anatomy, physiology, physical culture, hygiene, and "other topics relative to the laws of life and health" (Hitchcock, 1879, p. 5), took anthropometric measurements of them, measured arm strength, and established the first organized intramural athletic programs in this country. It was logical that when Dr. William Anderson called his friends and colleagues together at Adelphi College in 1885 to form the Association for the Advancement of Physical Education, Dr. Hitchcock was elected its first president. He proudly wrote,

> The fact that physical education is placed on an equality of position with each of the other departments, and contributes to a recognition of the character and standing of the student in the college records, is probably its most striking feature as an educational measure. It is thus an indication that health and physical exercise are of prime importance. (Hitchcock, 1879)

Dudley A. Sargent (1849-1924) joined a gymnastics club while in high school in Belfast, Maine. He was gymnastics instructor for 2 years at Bowdoin College before entering it as a freshman, and became director of gymnastics at Yale while still an undergraduate. After graduating from Yale Medical School in 1878, he established a private gymnasium in New York where he developed mechanical appliances for strength training and developed a system of body measurements he had started at Bowdoin and Yale under the influence of Hitchcock. When the Hemenway Gymnasium was opened at Harvard in 1880, he was appointed director and assistant professor. All freshmen were measured according to his system and were given strength tests.

During his 40 years in that position he accumulated thousands of measurements, founded a gymnastic training institution for young women which later became Radcliffe College, and in 1904 published his influential book *Health, Strength and Power* (Sargent, 1904). In urging the necessity of regular vigorous exercise for health, he cited the experience during the Civil War when more than half the men drafted from the professional classes and more than 40% from the mercantile and laboring classes were rejected because of physical disability and disease. He described and illustrated a series of exercises for children and men of all ages to achieve physical fitness without the use of machines.

William G. Anderson (1860-1947) became director of physical education at the Cleveland Medical College and received his MD there in 1883. After a year as director of Adelphia Academy, he founded the Brooklyn Normal School for Physical Education in 1886; in 1892 he became associate director of the Yale gymnasium. He also established the New Haven Normal School of Gymnastics in 1901 and enjoyed a long career and achieved national recognition in the field of physical education.

R. Tait McKenzie (1867-1938) was a Canadian who took his undergraduate and medical degrees at McGill University. Following graduation, internship, and a short period in private medical practice, he returned to McGill as a lecturer in anatomy and later became Medical Director of Physical Education. He moved to the University of Pennsylvania in 1904, becoming professor of physical education and director of the department. In 1909 he published *Exercise in Education and Medicine*, in which he described the physiological basis for exercise, discussed European systems of physical training, and reviewed the current status of physical education in this country. He also described physical education for handicapped persons. The second half of the book discussed the applications of exercise to pathologic conditions, establishing the foundation for what we now know as Physical Medicine and Rehabilitation.

With the onset of World War I McKenzie offered his services to the Canadian Armed Forces and was sent to England in 1915. He organized a system of physical training for convalescent soldiers and studied those who had been referred for treatment of heart disorders. Following the war he returned to the University of Pennsylvania, where he was Director of Physical Education until 1931. McKenzie's influence remained profound and was emphasized by his remarkable talent as a sculptor in reproducing the human form in all phases of effort and stress. He freely acknowledged his debt to Hitchcock, Sargent, Hartwell, McCurdy and all his predecessors and contemporaries. His work and career summed up what they had all believed and taught.

What we have learned, and what we know now about the relationship between exercise and the establishment, maintenance, and restoration of health, fills thousands of printed pages. It is no small tribute to the powers of human observation and reasoning that much of this, as technically oriented as it may be, simply confirms what our predecessors in education and medicine have learned and taught for several thousand years. We have built on the foundation they have laid down; we honor and we thank them.

REFERENCES

d'ACQUAPENDENTE, F. *De motu animalium.* 1614.

ADAMS, F. *Paulus Aegineta, the seven books of.* London, 1844.

ALDOBRANDINUS, U. *De quadripedibus.* 1616.

ANDRY, N. *L'Orthopedie, ou l'art de prevenir et corriger dans les enfants les difformites du corps.* 1741.

ASCLEPIADES, his life and writing (R.M. Green, Trans.). New Haven: Yale University Press, 1955.

BARBARO, F. *De re uxoria.* 1548.

BELL, J. *On regimen and longevity.* Philadelphia, 1842.

CLIAS, P. *Cours elementaire de gymnastique.* Paris, 1819.

DEUSING, A. *Exercitationes de motu animalium.* 1656.

DEWEES, W.P. *A treatise on the physical and medical treatment of children.* Philadelphia, 1826.

DUCHESNE, J. *Ars medica dogmatica-hermetica.* 1648.

EBERLE, J. *A treatise on the diseases and physical education of children.* Cincinnati, 1833.

FULLER, F. *Medicina gymnastica or a treatise concerning the power of exercise with respect to the animal economy and the great necessity of it in the course of several distempers.* London: Robert Knaplock, 1704.

GALEN, C. *De sanitate tuenda* (R.M. Green, Trans.). Springfield, IL: C.C. Thomas, 1951.

GUTHRIE, D. *A history of medicine.* London, 1945.

HACKENSMITH, C.W. *History of physical education.* New York: Harper & Row, 1966.

HITCHCOCK, E. *The department of physical education and hygiene Amherst College.* Boston: 1879.

HITCHCOCK, E., & Hitchcock, E., Jr. *Elementary anatomy and physiology for colleges, academies and other schools.* New York: 1860.

JOSEPH, L.H. *Gymnastics from the Middle Ages to the 18th Century.* Ciba Symposia 10:5, March-April 1949. Summit, NJ.

JOUBERT, L. *Opera.* 1582.

LeCLERC, D. *Histoire de la medicine.* 1723.

LITTRE, E. *Oeuvres completes d'Hippocrate.* Paris, 1839-1861.

MAIMONIDES, M. *Treatise on a hygiene.* 1199.

McCORMICK, P.F. *Two medieval Catholic educators (Vittorino da Feltre).* Catholic University Bulletin, vols. 12 and 13, 1943-1944.

McKENZIE, R. *Exercise in education and medicine.* Philadelphia: W.B. Saunders, 1909.

MERCURIALE, H. *De arte gymnastica.* 1569.

NENCI, G. *Discorsi sopra la ginnastica e sopra l'utilita dell' osservazione nella medicina practica.* 1766.

PALMIERI, M. *Libro della vita civile.* Giornale storico di lettere Italiane, 1894.

PARE, A. *Opera.* 1582.

PERRAULT, C. *Mecanique des animaux.* 1680.

PETRARCA, F. *Opera.* 1354.

PLATNER, J.Z. *De arte gymnastica veterum.* 1734.

ROSS, W.C. (Ed.). *The works of Aristotle.* 12 vols. Oxford: Oxford University Press, 1928-1952.

RUNES, D. *Selected writings of Benjamin Rush.* New York: Philosophical Library, 1947.

SARGENT, D.A. *Health, strength & power.* New York: Dodge, 1904.

SHRYOCK, R.H. Sylvester Graham and the popular health movement, 1830-1870. *Mississippi Valley Historical Review,* **18**, 172, 1931.

TAYLOR, G. *The Swedish movement cure.* New York, 1860.

TISSOT, C.J. *Gymnastique medicinale et chirurgicale.* 1780.

TUCCARO, S.A. *Tros dialogues de l'exercice de sauter et voltiger en l'air.* 1589.

VEGIUS, M. *De educatione librorum.* 1613.

VIVES, J.L. *De disciplinis.* 1536.

WESTERBLAD, C.A. *Ling, the founder of Swedish gymnastics.* London, 1909.

Exercise and Risk
of Coronary Heart Disease

Arthur S. Leon
University of Minnesota

RISK FACTORS ASSOCIATED
WITH CORONARY HEART DISEASE

Despite a recent decline, coronary heart disease remains the main cause of death in adults in the United States and other Western industrialized countries. Prospective epidemiologic studies over the past 30 years have shown that CHD has a multifactorial etiology (Kannel & Gordon, 1976; Keys, 1970, 1980; Pooling Project Research Group, 1978). Risk factors for the disease include biological and metabolic characteristics and certain living habits. Biological factors that increase host susceptibility and cannot be modified are age, male sex, and a strong family history of premature CHD.

Physiologic and Metabolic Risk Factors

Blood Lipid and Lipoprotein Levels. The severity of atherosclerosis and risk of CHD increases progressively with blood levels of total cholesterol and its principal lipoprotein carrier, low density lipoprotein (LDL). Experimentally LDL appears to be directly involved in the atherosclerotic process (Probstfield & Gotto, 1982). In contrast, both retrospective and prospective epidemiologic studies from diverse regions of the world show a strong inverse relationship between levels of plasma high density lipoprotein cholesterol (HDL-C) levels, which make up 20 to 30% of plasma total cholesterol, and risk of CHD (Gordon, 1978; WHO Expert Committee, 1982, p. 15). CHD cases generally had significantly lower HDL-C levels compared to people of the same age and sex without CHD. Prospective studies usually showed fairly large differences in incidence of CHD with differences at baseline of about 4 mg/dl HDL-C levels (Gordon, 1978). The HDL_2 subfraction may be the protective factor but this needs further confirmation (Probstfield & Gotto, 1982). Experimentally HDL is a lipid scavenger involved in reverse transport of cholesterol from the peripheral tissues to the liver, and it may also interfere with

LDL cholesterol cellular uptake (Carew, Hayes, Koschinsky, & Stein-berg, 1976; Levy & Rifkind, 1980). The Lower levels of total and LDL cholesterol levels in women until after the menopause and higher levels of HDL-C from adolescence onward most likely contribute to their lower risk of CHD as compared to men.

Neither plasma triglycerides nor their principal carrier in the fasting state, very low density lipoprotein (VLDL), appear to be independent risk factors (Hulley, Rosenman, Bawdl, & Brand, 1980; Probstfield & Gotto, 1982). However, they may indirectly play a role in the atherosclerotic process, since triglyceride levels are inversely related to HDL-C, and VLDL is the precursor of LDL.

Blood Pressure. Blood pressure is another major risk factor for CHD. It is also the principal risk factor for stroke due to atherosclerosis of cerebral arteries. Risk increases with levels of both systolic and diastolic blood pressure (Pooling Project Research Group, 1978; WHO Expert Committee, 1982, p. 23).

Diabetes Mellitus. Diabetes is a potent risk factor for CHD as well as for other cardiovascular problems (Leon, 1982; WHO Expert Com-mittee, 1982, p. 31). Acceleration of the atherosclerotic process is at-tributed to the elevated blood sugar itself, and to high blood insulin levels commonly found in obese, maturity-onset diabetics with cellular insulin insensitivity. Diabetics also generally have higher blood pressure and more frequent blood lipid abnormalities (elevated cholesterol and triglyceride levels and decreased HDL-C levels) than nondiabetics (Leon, 1982).

Obesity. Although overweight does not appear to be an indepen-dent risk factor for CHD, it may potentiate other risk factors (WHO Ex-pert Committee, 1982, p. 30). These include blood lipid abnormalities (increases in total cholesterol and triglyceride and a reduction in HDL-C levels), an increase in blood pressure, and disturbances in glucose metab-olism, that is, glucose intolerance, cellular insulin insensitivity, or frank maturity-onset diabetes in those with a genetic predisposition.

Living Habits Increasing CHD Risk

Modern Western Diet. The modern Western diet is an important if not essential factor contributing to mass CHD (Blackburn, 1979; WHO Ex-pert Committee, 1982, p. 14). Excess calorie intake relative to physical activity causes obesity. Common sources of excess calories are dietary fat, sugar, and alcohol. In addition, cultures in which at least 15% of calories are obtained from saturated fat (mostly from animal sources), are subject to mass hypercholesteremia and elevated levels of LDL-C. A coincident low intake of complex carbohydrates and dietary fiber may be a small additional contributor to the elevated blood cholesterol. A high salt intake in a population is invariably associated with an increased prevalence of essential hypertension.

Cigarette Smoking. Cigarette smoking is a principal causative factor for CHD (Kannel & Gordon, 1976; Pooling Project Research Group, 1978; WHO Expert Committee, 1982, p. 26). Multiple mechanisms appear to be involved. These include increased catecholamine release caused by nicotine (which in turn increases heart work and irritability), elevated carboxyhemoglobin levels, decreased HDL-C levels, and accelerated atherosclerosis.

Stress (Coronary-Prone Behavior). A constellation of behavioral traits collectively called coronary prone or Type A behavior have been demonstrated to independently increase CHD risk (Dembroski & Feinleib, 1977; Review Panel on Coronary-Prone Behavior and Coronary Heart Disease, 1981; Rosenman et al., 1975; WHO Expert Committee, 1982, p. 32). These traits include excess competitiveness, impatience, hostility, constant-time pressure, multiphasic thinking, and rapid, forceful speech. An excess secretion of catecholamines in response to stress in Type A's is postulated to accelerate atherosclerosis. No data are available on what effect a reversal of this behavioral pattern has on rate of CHD events, nor is there currently any effective strategy for reversing it.

Alcohol Intake. Moderate use of alcohol has repeatedly been shown in epidemiologic studies to be associated with a lower CHD incidence as compared to abstinence (WHO Expert Committee, 1982, p. 33). This may be related at least partially to its ability to raise HDL-C (Willett, Hennekens, Siegel, Adner, & Castello, 1980). In contrast, heavy use of alcohol (75 grams or about 5 drinks per day) may have a causal role in obesity and hypertension, and is associated with a significant increase in CHD rate.

Physical Inactivity. Another hallmark of the modern lifestyle that may be related to CHD is inactivity. This results from mass mechanization and automation on the job, dependence on motorized transportation, labor-saving devices in the home, and predominantly passive leisure-time pursuits. During the past 30 or so years, epidemiologists have investigated how a sedentary lifestyle contributes to mass atherosclerosis and associated CHD risk. Results of epidemiologic studies on selected industries, regional population samples, insurance plans, and athletes versus nonathletes and former college students have generally supported the hypothesis, particularly recent studies that have considered leisure-time exercise (Blackburn, 1983; Fletcher, 1982; Froelicher, 1983; Leon & Blackburn, 1981). The inverse relationship found between resting pulse rate and CHD events supports the hypothesis, since a negative correlation exists between heart rate and physical fitness level. In these population studies, physical inactivity is commonly associated with obesity, elevated blood pressure, abnormal blood lipids, glucose intolerance, diabetes mellitus, and cigarette smoking.

Recent studies have corrected for at least some of these confounding variables and, although diminished, the apparent protective effect of exercise persists. However, these studies are inconclusive due to the problems of self-selection, inaccuracies in measuring habitual physical activity, and absence of a definitive large-scale exercise primary prevention trial. Furthermore, it is clear particularly from Scandinavian studies such as the Finnish cohort in the Seven Countries Collaborative Study (Keys, 1980) that physical inactivity is less potent a risk factor than levels of blood cholesterol and blood pressure, cigarette smoking, and diet. Protective effects of exercise appear to be overwhelmed by high levels of these other risk factors.

Vigorous physical activity may help protect against CHD through direct and indirect influences on several risk factors contributing to atherogenesis. In fact, it is difficult to distinguish the independent effects of regular endurance exercise from the effects of associated weight loss on risk factors. This has been a research interest in the Minnesota Laboratory of Physiological Hygiene. Summarized below is some of the evidence of direct and indirect effects of endurance exercise on other coronary risk factors, beginning with its influence on body weight.

EXERCISE AND OBESITY

Population studies show that physically active people are generally leaner than inactive people despite eating more as a group (Kannel & Gordon, 1976; Keys, 1970). An inverse relationship also has been demonstrated between maximal oxygen uptake, an index of physical fitness, and relative weight (Cantwell, Watt, & Piper, 1979; Leon, Jacobs, DeBacker, & Taylor, 1981). Experimentally exercise has been demonstrated effective in weight reduction even with ad libitum food intake (Leon, Conrad, Hunninghake, & Serfass, 1979). Several mechanisms have been proposed to explain this (Leon & Blackburn, 1983). In addition to the direct energy requirements for physical effort, evidence suggests that resting metabolic rate continues elevated for hours following endurance activities, but this remains to be confirmed. Exercise also is postulated to more adequately adjust appetite signals, and it certainly can divert one from snacking. In addition, weight loss from exercise involves a greater reduction in body fat than dieting, and preserves or increases lean body tissues, which are often sacrificed during dieting. As previously mentioned, weight reduction with exercise may be responsible for, or at least contribute significantly to, the effects of exercise on other risk factors including blood lipids, blood pressure, and glucose intolerance (Blackburn, 1983).

EXERCISE AND BLOOD LIPIDS

Physical Fitness vs. Blood Lipids

Several approaches have been used to assess the relationship of physical activity to blood lipids. One approach considers the correlation between blood lipid concentrations and physical fitness, as measured by treadmill duration or maximal oxygen uptake in systematic population samples or selected groups of individuals (Haskell, Taylor, Wood, Schmitt, & Heiss, 1980; Huttunen, 1982). Significant but weak negative correlations have been observed between levels of both serum cholesterol and triglycerides and maximal oxygen uptake. In other words, as physical fitness increased these blood lipids decreased. However, when adjustments were made for age and relative weight or body fatness, the relationships were usually lost, suggesting that the effect of physical fitness on blood lipids acted through these other variables rather than having an independent influence.

Few studies have explored the relationship between plasma lipoprotein levels and indicators of physical fitness. A positive correlation between physical fitness and HDL-C levels has been reported, that is, the more marked the fitness, the higher the HDL-C. However, the recent Lipid Research Clinics Prevalence Program Study (Haskell et al., 1980) was unable to find a significant relationship when adjustments were made for other factors affecting HDL-C concentration such as relative weight, alcohol intake, and cigarette smoking. The authors suggested that a causal link between physical activity and HDL-C may operate through a process other than physical fitness. In addition, studies in the Minnesota Laboratory of Physiological Hygiene indicate that treadmill duration and maximal oxygen uptake are related to factors other than recent physical activity or exercise, and that in a general population only 10 to 25% of the variation in treadmill performance can be accounted for by self-reports of recent exercise habits (Leon et al., 1981; Taylor, Jacobs, Schucker, Knudsen, Leon, & DeBacker, 1978).

Physical Activity vs. Blood Lipids

Another approach has been to compare directly in population groups indices of physical activity derived from self-reports of work and/or recreational activities with blood lipid and lipoprotein levels. Using this approach, a physically active lifestyle seems to be consistently associated with a favorable lipid lipoprotein profile (Haskell et al., 1980; Huttunen, 1982; Lehtonen, 1982; Montoye, Block, Metzner, & Keller, 1976). Several reports showed that plasma triglycerides and VLDL concentrations were generally lower in subjects who were vigorously active as compared to more sedentary counterparts; however, the more active subjects were also generally leaner. In the Tecumseh Community Study, Montoye and colleagues (1976) found that the difference in triglyceride levels between the most and least active subjects was lost after correcting for body fatness. Studies on the relationship between physical activity levels and serum total cholesterol have yielded conflicting results. In the Tecumseh Study (Montoye et al., 1976), serum cholesterol was lower in the most active as compared to the least active subjects; however, as with triglycerides, the differences disappeared when the investigators corrected for body fatness.

Both population studies and cross-sectional comparisons of endurance athletes with nonathletes have consistently reported higher concentrations of HDL-C in the more active subjects. In the Lipid Research Clinic Program Prevalence Study (Haskell et al., 1980), both men and women who reported some strenuous exercise had significantly higher HDL-C levels than their sedentary counterparts. The differences were independent of other factors influencing HDL-C concentration. Furthermore, men and women who have been endurance athletes for years such as joggers, marathon runners, cross-country skiers, and swimmers have HDL-C levels 10 to 40% higher than matched sedentary controls (Farrell, Maksud, Pollock, Foster, Anolm, Hare, & Leon, 1982; Hartung, Forteyt, Mitchell, Vlasek, & Gotto, 1980; Haskell et al., 1980; Huttunen, 1982; Lehtonen, 1982; Lehtonen & Viikari, 1978; Rotkis, Cote, Coyle, & Wilmore, 1982; Smith, Mendez, Drukenmiller, & Kris-Etherton, 1982; Wood, Haskell, Stern, Lewis, & Perry, 1977).

For runners, a significant stepwise increase in HDL-C levels was found with increases in mileage run from 10 to 40 or more miles per week (Rotkis et al., 1982). Sports involving high intensity, anaerobic activity such as sprinting, or isometric activities such as weight-lifting, did not affect HDL-C (Farrell et al., 1982; Rotkis et al., 1982). Many earlier studies did not adjust HDL-C levels for measurements of adiposity, cigarette smoking, diet, or alcohol consumption; however, these confounding variables have been considered in more recent studies and the relationship with physical activity, although diminished, has persisted (Hartung et al., 1980; Haskell et al., 1980; Rotkis et al., 1982; Willett, Hennekens, Castelli, Rosner, Evans, Taylor, & Kass, 1983). In addition, preadolescent and young adult athletes had higher HDL-C levels than nonathletes of similar leanness (Thorland & Gilliam, 1981).

Exercise Training Experiments

Conclusive evidence of the effects of physical activity on blood lipids requires controlled exercise training experiments. Conflicting results have been obtained from such studies. These differences reflect variations in the following: composition of the study populations and control group;

the exercise training programs including type of exercise, intensity, duration, and frequency of sessions and length of training; accuracy of measurement procedures; baseline levels of lipids; initial and final physical fitness, body weight, dietary habits, and alcohol and cigarette use; seasonal fluctuations in lipid levels; and probably other factors. The direct effects of exercise (generally walk-jog programs) on serum cholesterol levels are inconclusive, with either reductions or no change reported (Fletcher, 1982, p. 114; Huttunen, 1982; Lopez-S, 1976).

There also have been mixed results from studies on the effects of endurance exercise training on HDL-C levels. Most exercise training studies in young and middle-aged men have shown an increase in HDL-C and/or HDL/LDL ratio (Brownell, Bachorik, & Ayerle, 1982; Hartung, Squires, & Gotto, 1981; Haskell et al., 1980; Huttunen, 1982; Huttunen, Lansimies, Voutilaines, Hietnaen, Penttila, Siitonen, & Rauramaa, 1979; Leon et al., 1979; Lopez-S, 1976; Sopko, Leon, Jacobs, Foster, & Moy, 1982; Williams, Wood, Haskell, & Vranizan, 1982; Wood, Haskell, Blair, Williams, Krauss, Lindgren, Albers, Ping, & Farquhar, 1983; Casal, Leon, Moy, Shaw, McNally, & Hughes, 1983). Recent studies in the Minnesota Laboratory of Physiological Hygiene have found these changes can occur in the absence of associated weight loss (Sopko et al., 1982; Casal et al., in press). In contrast, Lipson, Bonow, Schaefer, Brewer, and Lindgren (1980) found no change in HDL-C in a group of men who exercised 6 weeks with weight and diet composition kept constant on a metabolic ward. The few training studies including women have failed to show any effect on HDL-C levels even in the presence of weight loss (Brownell et al., 1982).

Williams and colleagues (1982) in a recent long-term, large-scale study reported that at least 10 miles per week of running for 9 months was required to significantly raise HDL-C levels in men in the presence of only a slight decrease in body weight and fat. Our group found a mean increase of about 16% above baseline levels for HDL-C with 24 miles per week of brisk treadmill walking (3.2 miles per hour at a 10% grade, 5 days per week) for 16 weeks in 6 obese young men. This resulted in a considerable loss of body weight and fat (Leon et al., 1979). In a recent controlled feeding experiment in our laboratory, 3,500 kcal a week of brisk treadmill walking (about 20 miles per week) for 12 weeks with or without an associated weight loss was effective in raising HDL-C in obese young men (Sopko et al., 1982). The group that lost weight during the exercise program had a 28% increase in HDL-C as compared to a 10% increase in the group whose weight was held constant, and an 8% increase in those who lost weight by dieting. Similarly Casal et al. (1983) in our laboratory observed a 12% increase in HDL-C in a group of men who climbed 50 flights of stairs and walked 12 miles per week on a treadmill for 12 weeks with weight remaining constant.

A proposed mechanism for the HDL-C and triglyceride changes with exercise in addition to weight and fat loss is through an associated increase in peripheral tissue lipoprotein lipase activity (Huttunen, 1982; Lopez-S, 1976). A breakdown of plasma VLDL by lipoprotein lipase is believed to contribute to plasma HDL levels. It is concluded that a formal program of regular endurance activities such as running or brisk walking has a favorable influence on blood lipid levels, particularly an increase in HDL-C. This increase in HDL with exercise training appears to be primarily in the HDL_2 subfraction (Wood et al., 1983). There appears to be a synergistic effect of exercise and weight loss on HDL-C levels, at least in men.

EXERCISE AND BLOOD PRESSURE

Epidemiological Studies

Whether or not resting blood pressure level is related to habitual physical activity and whether inactivity is a cause of hypertension is difficult to assess epidemiologically because of numerous confounding variables. Population studies in which blood pressure levels were compared cross-sectionally in men in physically demanding versus light occupations have yielded conflicting results. Blood pressure levels were either lower, the same, or higher in men performing physical labor as compared to less active workers (Leon & Blackburn, 1982; Montoye, 1975). The prevalence of esential hypertension in these studies appeared to be unrelated to physical activity on the job.

There are few longitudinal studies on the relationship of exercise habits or sports in youth to subsequent incidence of adult hypertension. Two such large-scale studies involving a 20-year follow-up of college alumni found a 20 to 40% greater incidence of physician-diagnosed hypertension in men who in college had reported less than 5 hours a week of exercise as compared to those who reported 5 or more hours a week of exercise (Gillum & Paffenbarger, 1978; Paffenbarger, Thome, & Wing, 1968). Population studies generally showed no relationship between blood pressure levels and vigorous leisure time activity or combined job and leisure time activity. An exception was the Tecumseh Community Study (Montoye, 1975), in which the more active men had significantly lower blood pressure levels at all ages; and an inverse relationship was found between daily energy expenditure and blood pressure levels. However, when adjustment was made by bivariate analysis for body fatness, the tendency for active people to have lower blood pressure was reduced. Fatness also was found to be a greater contributor to blood pressure elevation than physical inactivity. Some studies have shown an inverse relationship between blood pressure and physical fitness as determined by exercise testing, which was independent of body weight (Cooper, Pollock, Martin, White, Linnerud, & Jackson, 1976; Gyntelberg & Meyer, 1974). Several prospective studies also have found that hypertensives who exercise regularly have a lower probability of CHD events than those who remain inactive (Leon & Blackburn, 1982).

Experimental Studies

Studies on the effects of experimental exercise conditioning on blood pressure levels also have yielded inconsistent results (Kukkonen, Rauramaa, Voutilainen, & Lansimies, 1982; Leon & Blackburn, 1982). Such studies are as difficult to interpret as those evaluating the effects of exercise on blood lipid levels. An additional problem is that during the course of a study blood pressure reduction often occurs in the absence of intervention in both normotensives and hypertensives, because of familiarity due to frequent contact and repeated blood pressure determinations. This illustrates the need for a nontrained control group. Few studies have met this criterion. These few controlled studies have shown in both normotensives and hypertensive subjects either no significant change in blood pressure with training or a similar small blood pressure reduction in both the trained and control groups.

It is possible that a physically active lifestyle from youth on can reduce the incidence of future hypertension, but this remains to be confirmed by additional prospective studies. The principal effect of endurance exercise on resting blood pressure appears to be through an associated reduction in weight. There is little evidence of any clinically significant, independent effect of endurance exercise training on resting blood pressure, either in normotensive or hypertensive subjects. However, hypertensives who exercise regularly appear to have a lower risk of CHD events as compared to those who don't exercise. This could be related to reduced heart rate and myocardial oxygen requirements or associated blood lipid changes with training.

Recently, Stamler, Farinaro, Mojonnier, Hall, Moss, and Stamler (1980) showed in a long-term prospective study that exercise as part of a multifactor intervention program, including weight reduction and modified eating habits, could prevent development of hypertension among susceptible persons or could control mild hypertension.

EXERCISE AND DIABETES MELLITUS

Epidemiologic Studies

Epidemiologic studies indicate that physical inactivity is a risk factor for maturity-onset, noninsulin-dependent (Type II) diabetes mellitus

(Sullivan, 1982; West, 1978). Increased body weight is a contributing factor. The effects of endurance exercise on glucose metabolism, cellular sensitivity to insulin, and diabetic control have recently been reviewed (Leon, 1982; Sullivan, 1982). An increase in rate of glucose utilization occurs during acute exercise in both diabetics and nondiabetics, and persists for hours or days after exercise cessation during resynthesis of depleted tissue glycogen stores. Enhanced cellular sensitivity to insulin also occurs with prolonged endurance exercise. During exercise training, these acute effects act in conjunction with reduced weight and fat stores, and an increase in number of insulin receptors, to lower the plasma insulin concentration and improve glucose tolerance in obese people. This should help prevent clinical diabetes. For example, we observed a 43% reduction below baseline levels in blood insulin to glucose ratio following an oral glucose challenge in a group of obese young men after exercise training and an associated 12-lb. weight loss (Leon et al., 1979).

We also studied the effects of moderate intensity walking exercise, 2 to 4 hours per week, with body weight held constant on diabetic control and blood lipid levels in mild to moderately severe, Type II diabetics (Leon, Conrad, Casal, & Goetz, 1980). Under these conditions, no significant improvement in diabetic control or in the blood lipid profile followed training. Thus, exercise at the level used in our study apparently is insufficient by itself to control diabetes; it should be used instead in conjunction with appropriate dietary changes, weight normalization and, if necessary, insulin to achieve control. In insulin dependent (Type I) diabetics with mild or moderate hyperglycemia, regular exercise enhances diabetic control and reduces exogenous insulin requirements. However, exercise may be detrimental in the presence of markedly uncontrolled diabetes, particularly if ketosis is present.

EXERCISE AND CIGARETTE SMOKING, ALCOHOL CONSUMPTION, AND OTHER HEALTH HABITS

A lower mortality rate from CHD has been reported in physically active smokers, as compared to inactive smokers (Hammond, 1964; Shapiro, Weinblatt, Frank, & Sager, 1969). Anecdotally, regular exercise reportedly reverses poor health habits such as cigarette smoking, improper diet, and excess alcohol intake. However, no well controlled, long-term studies confirm these associations. For example, middle-aged American and Finnish men at high risk for CHD who took part in an 18-month exercise program made only temporary changes in lifestyle habits (Ilmarinen & Fardy, 1977; Taylor, Buskirk, & Remington, 1972). These disappeared by the end of the 18-month intervention in the American study. A 3-year follow-up in the Finnish study likewise showed no significant changes from baseline in current exercise or other lifestyle habits, including smoking and alcohol use. Smoking and chronic cough also have recently been reported to be independent factors contributing to *nonadherence* to exercise programs following a heart attack (Oldridge, Doitner, Buck, Jones, Andrew, Parker, Cunningham, Kavanagh, Rechnitzer, & Sutton, 1983).

EXERCISE AND CORONARY-PRONE BEHAVIOR

In the Western Collaborative Study no relationship was found between habitual physical activity levels and coronary-prone (Type A) behavior (Rosenman et al., 1975). Although there are reports that exercise can reduce manifestations of stress and muscular tension, this is difficult to document; it is also unknown whether such changes will reduce the incidence of CHD (Leon, 1972; Leon & Blackburn, 1982). Recently Haskell and Wood noted a slight reduction in Type A characteristics in men after exercise training (personal communication). This needs to be confirmed.

In addition to effects on risk factors, hemodynamic adaptations to regular endurance exercise have been demonstrated experimentally, which probably contribute to protective effects of exercise against CHD. These have been extensively reviewed elsewhere and will be only briefly summarized below (Amsterdam, Laslett, Dressendorfer, & Mason, 1981; Fletcher, 1982, p. 103; Froelicher, 1983; Leon, 1972; Leon & Blackburn, 1982; Leon & Bloor, 1975; Shephard, 1981, p. 66).

EXERCISE AND MYOCARDIAL VASCULARITY

Animal studies have shown that endurance exercise can enlarge the main coronaries, and increase coronary collateral vessels and the myocardial capillary density. In a recent landmark study, Kramsch, Aspen, Abramowitz, Kreimendahl, and Hood (1981) found that monkeys on an isocaloric, atherogenic diet for 36 to 43 weeks who jogged regularly on a treadmill had larger coronary arteries and hearts, and less coronary atherosclerosis and stenosis than nonexercise controls. In addition, HDL-C levels were higher in the exercise group and ischemic ECG changes on exercise tests and sudden death were noted only in sedentary monkeys. These cardiovascular findings are consistent with human postmortem findings that physically active men have larger coronary arteries, fewer coronary occlusions, and less myocardial ischemic damage than inactive men. However, in most human studies similar amounts of atherosclerosis were found in the active and inactive men.

OTHER ADAPTIVE PHYSIOLOGIC CHANGES
WITH EXERCISE

Other important physiologic adaptive changes result from exercise training that may help protect against heart attacks. A reduced heart rate at rest and during exercise is an early effect of endurance exercise training. Since heart rate is an important determinant of myocardial oxygen requirements, this adaptation to exercise is especially important in the presence of advanced coronary artery disease, such as in patients with angina pectoris or after a myocardial infarction. The associated longer diastolic interval also increases coronary perfusion of the subendocardial region of the heart. Exercise training may significantly reduce systolic blood pressure during submaximal levels of exercise even if it does not alter resting blood pressure. This further reduces myocardial oxygen requirements and the possibility of ischemia in the presence of coronary atherosclerosis.

Other reported direct cardiac effects of exercise training in normal individuals include increases in maximal stroke volume, cardiac output, cardiac size chamber volume, and ejection fraction—in other words, a functional improvement of the heart as a pump. Peripheral adaptations reported with training can indirectly improve the efficiency of the heart and further reduce myocardial oxygen demands. Chronically exercised skeletal muscles show an increase in number and size of mitochondria and activity of their enzymes. Other adaptations include increases in the following: ATPase activity, the rate of aerobic metabolism of many substrates, myoglobin concentration, and muscle capillary density. These adaptations increase the arteriovenous oxygen difference and maximal oxygen uptake of the body and decrease muscle blood flow during exercise. An increase in oxygen-carrying capacity of the blood and improved ability of the red blood cells to release oxygen may further contribute to the increased arteriovenous oxygen difference with training.

CONCLUSIONS AND SUMMARY

Coronary heart disease, the No. 1 health problem in Western life, is caused by an interaction of multiple factors. While physical inactivity does not appear to be a major cause, it contributes to hemodynamic and metabolic changes that aggravate the underlying atherosclerotic process and unfavorably disturb the balance between myocardial oxygen supply and demand. Perhaps the most important mechanism for the partial protective effect of regular endurance activities against CHD is by reducing fat stores and body weight. This in turn favorably alters several major etiologic factors for atherogenesis. These include blood lipids with a reduction in plasma total and LDL cholesterol and an increase in HDL cholesterol, a decrease in blood pressure, and improved glucose-insulin metabolism. There also appears to be a significant direct effect of regular endurance exercise on HDL cholesterol and cellular insulin sensitivity.

Peripheral and central hemodynamic adaptations with chronic endurance exercise, particularly heart rate reduction and skeletal muscle adaptations, favorably affect the myocardial oxygen supply/demand balance. These adaptations improve cardiovascular efficiency and should help protect the heart against ischemia even in the presence of severe atherosclerosis. Finally, although there remains scientific uncertainty and controversy over the value of endurance exercise in prevention of CHD, there is no question about its beneficial effects as part of a hygienic pattern of living on general physical and mental well-being.

REFERENCES

AMSTERDAM, E.A., Laslett, L.J., Dressendorfer, R.H., & Mason, D.T. Exercise training in coronary heart disease: Is there a cardiac effect? *American Heart Journal*, 1981, **101**, 870-873.

BLACKBURN, H. Diet and mass hyperlipidemia: A public health view. In R. Levy, B.M. Rifkind, B. Dennis, & N.D. Ernst (Eds.), *Nutrition, lipids and coronary heart disease*. New York: Raven Press, 1979.

BLACKBURN, H. Physical activity and coronary heart disease: A brief update and population view. *Journal of Cardiac Rehabilitation*, 1983, **3**, 101-111; 171-174.

BROWNELL, K.D., Bachorik, P.S., & Ayerle, R.S. Changes in plasma lipid and lipoprotein levels in men and women after a program of moderate exercise. *Circulation*, 1982, **65**, 477-484.

CANTWELL, J., Watt, E.W., & Piper, J.H., Jr. Fitness, aerobic points, and coronary risk. *Physician and Sportsmedicine*, 1979, **7**, 79-84.

CAREW, T.E., Hayes, S.B., Koschinsky, T., & Steinberg, D. A mechanism by which high-density lipoprotein may slow the atherogenic process. *Lancet*, 1976, **1**, 1315-1317.

CASAL, D.C., Leon, A.S., Moy, J., Shaw, G., McNally, C., & Hughes, J. Effects of 2000 KCAL per week of treadmill walking and stairclimbing on coronary risk factors. *Medicine Science in Sports and Exercise*, 1983, **15**. (abstract)

COOPER, K., Pollock, M.L., Martin, R.P., White, S.R., Linnerud, A.C., & Jackson, A. Physical fitness levels and selected risk factors. A cross-sectional study. *Journal of the American Medical Association*, 1976, **236**, 166-169.

DEMBROSKI, T., & Feinleib, M. (Eds.), *Proceedings of the Forum of Coronary-Prone Behavior*. (DHEW Publication [NIH] No. 78-1451). Washington, DC: US Government Printing Office, 1977.

FARRELL, P.A., Maksud, M.G., Pollock, M.L., Foster, C., Anolm, J., Hare, J., & Leon, A.S. A comparison of plasma cholesterol, triglycerides, and high density lipoprotein cholesterol in speed skaters, weight lifters, and non-athletes. *European Journal of Applied Physiology*, 1982, **48**, 77-82.

FLETCHER, G.F. *Exercise in the practice of medicine*. Mount Kisco, NY: Futura, 1982.

FROELICHER, V. *Exercise testing and training*. New York: LeJacq, 1983.

GILLUM, R.F., & Paffenbarger, R.S., Jr. Chronic disease in former college students. XVII. Sociocultural mobility as a precursor of coronary heart disease and hypertension. *American Journal of Epidemiology*, 1978, **108**, 289-298.

GORDON, T. High density lipoprotein and atherosclerosis: Comments on the epidemiologic background. In A.M. Grotto, Jr., N.E. Miller, & M.F. Oliver (Eds.), *High density lipoproteins and atherosclerosis*. New York: Elsevier/North-Holland Biomedical Press, 1978.

GYNTELBERG, F., & Meyer, J. Relationship between blood pressure and physical fitness, smoking, and alcohol consumption in Copenhagen males aged 40-59. *Acta Medica Scandinavica*, 1974, **195**, 375-380.

HAMMOND, E.C. Smoking in relationship to morbidity and mortality: Findings in the first thirty-four months of follow-up in a prospective study staged in 1959. *Journal of the National Cancer Institute*, 1964, **32**, 1161-1188.

HARTUNG, G.H., Forteyt, J.P., Mitchell, R.E., Vlasek, I., & Gotto, A.M., Jr. Relationship of diet to high-density-lipoprotein cholesterol in middle-aged marathon runners, joggers, and inactive men. *New England Journal of Medicine*, 1980, **302**, 356-361.

HARTUNG, G.H., Squires, W.G., & Gotto, A.M., Jr. Effect of exercise training on plasma high-density lipoprotein cholesterol in coronary disease patients. *American Heart Journal*, 1981, **101**, 181-184.

HASKELL, W.L., Taylor, H.L., Wood, P.D., Schmitt, H., & Heiss, G. Strenuous physical activity, treadmill exercise test performance and plasma high-density-lipoprotein cholesterol. The Lipid Research Clinics Program Prevalence Study. *Circulation*, 1980, **62** (Suppl.), IV53-IV61.

HULLEY, S., Rosenman, R., Bawdl, R., & Brand, R. Epidemiology as a guide to clinical decisions: The association between triglycerides and coronary heart disease. *New England Journal of Medicine*, 1980, **302**, 1383-1389.

HUTTUNEN, J.K. Physical activity and plasma lipids and lipoprotein. *Annals of Clinical Research*, 1982, **14** (Suppl.), 124-129.

HUTTUNEN, J.K., Lansimies, E., Voutilaines, E.C., Hietnaen, E., Penttila, I., Siitonen, O., & Rauramaa, R. Effect of moderate physical exercise on serum lipoprotein. A controlled clinical trial with special reference to serum high-density lipoproteins. *Circulation*, 1979, **60**, 1220-1229.

ILMARINEN, J., & Fardy, P.S. Physical activity intervention for males. *Preventive Medicine*, 1977, **6**, 416-425.

KANNEL, W.B., & Gordon, T. (Eds.), *The Framingham Study—An epidemiological intervention of cardiovascular disease*. Section 31. Washington, DC: US Department of HEW, April 1976.

KEYS, A. (Ed.), Coronary heart disease in seven countries. *Circulation*, 1970, **41** (Suppl. 1). I1-I20.

KEYS, A. *Seven countries. A multivariate analysis of death and coronary heart disease*. Cambridge, MA: Harvard University Press, 1980.

KRAMSCH, D.M., Aspen, A.J., Abramowitz, B.M., Kreimendahl, T., & Hood, W.B., Jr. Reduction of coronary atherosclerosis by moderate conditioning exercise in monkeys on an atherogenic diet. *New England Journal of Medicine*, 1981, **305**, 1483-1488.

KUKKONEN, K., Rauramaa, R., Voutilainen, E.C., & Lansimies, E. Physical training of middle-aged men with borderline hypertension. *Annals of Clinical Research*, 1982, **14** (Suppl. 34), 139-145.

LEHTONEN, A. Exercise training and serum lipids. In E. Heitanen (Ed.), *Regulation of serum lipids by physical exercise*. Boca Raton, FL: CRC Press, 1982.

LEHTONEN, A., & Viikari, J. Serum triglycerides and cholesterol and serum high density lipoprotein cholesterol in highly physically active men. *Acta Medica Scandinavica*, 1978, **204**, 111-114.

LEON, A.S. Comparative cardiovascular adaptations to exercise in animals and man and its relevance to coronary heart disease. In C.M. Bloor (Ed.), *Comparative pathophysiology of circulatory diseases*. New York: Plenum, 1972.

LEON, A.S. The diabetic patient and athletic performance. In W. Haskell, J. Scala, & J. Whittam (Eds.), *Nutrition and athletic performance*. Palo Alto, CA: Bull Publ., 1982.

LEON, A.S., & Blackburn, H. Physical activity in the prevention of coronary heart disease: An update 1981. In B. Arnold, L.H. Kuller, & R. Greenlick (Eds.), *Advances in disease prevention* (Vol. 1). New York: Springer, 1981.

LEON, A.S., & Blackburn, H. Physical activity and hypertension. In P. Sleight & E.D. Freis (Eds.), *Butterworth international medical reviews. Cardiology 1. Hypertension*. London: Butterworth Scientific, 1982.

LEON, A.S., & Blackburn, H. Physical activity and coronary heart disease. In N. Kaplan & J. Stamler (Eds.), *Preventive cardiology*. Philadelphia: W.B. Saunders, 1983.

LEON, A.S., & Bloor, C.M. The effect of complete and partial deconditioning on exercise-induced cardiovascular changes in the rat. In V. Manninen & I. Halonen (Eds.), *Physical activity and coronary heart disease*. Basel: S. Karger, 1975.

LEON, A.S., Conrad, J., Casal, D.C., & Goetz, F. Failure of exercise alone to control maturity-onset diabetes. *Medicine and Science in Sports*, 1980, **12**, 104.

LEON, A.S., Conrad, J., Hunninghake, D.B., & Serfass, R. Effects of a vigorous walking program on body composition, and carbohydrate and lipid metabolism of obese young men. *American Journal of Clinical Nutrition*, 1979, **32**, 1776-1789.

LEON, A.S., Jacobs, D.R., Jr., DeBacker, G., & Taylor, H.L. Relationship of physical characteristics and life habits to treadmill exercise capacity. *American Journal of Epidemiology*, 1981, **113**, 653-660.

LEVY, R., & Rifkind, B.M. The structure, function, and metabolism of high density lipoproteins: A status report. *Circulation*, 1980, **62** (Suppl. 4), IV4-IV8.

LIPSON, L.C., Bonow, R.O., Schaefer, E.J., Brewer, H.B., & Lindgren, F.T. Effect of exercise conditioning on plasma high density lipoproteins. *Atherosclerosis*, 1980, **37**, 529-538.

LOPEZ-S, A. Effect of exercise on serum lipids and lipoproteins. In C.E. Day & R.S. Levy (Eds.), *Low density lipoproteins*. New York: Plenum, 1976.

MONTOYE, H.J. *Physical activity and health: An epidemiologic study of an entire community*. Englewood Cliffs, NJ: Prentice-Hall, 1975.

MONTOYE, H.J., Block, W.D., Metzner, H.L., & Keller, J.B. Habitual physical activity and serum lipids of males, age 16-64 in a total community. *Journal of Chronic Diseases*, 1976, **29**, 698-709.

OLDRIDGE, N.B., Doitner, A.P., Buck, C.W., Jones, N.L., Andrew, G.M., Parker, J.O., Cunningham, D.A., Kavanagh, T., Rechnitzer, P.A., & Sutton, J.R. Predictors of dropout from cardiac exercise rehabilitation. Ontario Exercise-Heart Collaborative Study. *American Journal of Cardiology*, 1983, **51**, 70-74.

PAFFENBARGER, R.S., Jr., Thome, M.C., & Wing, A.L. Chronic disease in former college students. VIII. Characteristics in youth disposing to hypertension in later life. *American Journal of Epidemiology*, 1968, **88**, 25-52.

POOLING Project Research Group. Relationship of blood pressure, serum cholesterol, smoking habit, relative weight, and ECG abnormalities to incidence of major coronary events: Final report of the Pooling Project. *Journal of Chronic Disease*, 1978, **31**, 201-306.

PROBSTFIELD, J.L., & Gotto, A.M., Jr. Lipoproteins in health and disease: Diagnosis and management. *Baylor College of Medicine Cardiology Series*, 1982, **5**, 1-31.

REVIEW Panel on Coronary-Prone Behavior and Coronary Heart Disease. Coronary-prone behavior and coronary heart disease: A critical review. *Circulation*, 1981, **63**, 1199-1215.

ROSENMAN, R.H., Brand, R.J., Jenkins, C.D., Friedman, M., Straus, R., & Wurm, M. Coronary heart disease in the western collaborative study: Final follow-up experience of 8½ years. *Journal of American Medical Association*, 1975, **233**, 872-877.

ROTKIS, T.C., Cote, R., Coyle, E., & Wilmore, J.H. Relationship between high density lipoprotein cholesterol and weekly running mileage. *Journal of Cardiac Rehabilitation*, 1982, **2**, 109-112.

SHAPIRO, S., Weinblatt, E., Frank, C.W., & Sager, R.V. Incidence of coronary heart disease in a population insured for medical care (HIP). Myocardial infarction, angina pectoris and possible myocardial infarction. *American Journal of Public Health*, 1969, **59**, (Suppl. 2), 1-101.

SHEPHARD, R.J. *Ischaemic heart disease and exercise*. Chicago: Croom Holm, 1981.

SMITH, M.P., Mendez, J., Drukenmiller, M., & Kris-Etherton, P.M. Exercise intensity, dietary intake, and high density lipoprotein cholesterol in young female competitive swimmers. *American Journal of Clinical Nutrition*, 1982, **36**, 251-257.

SOPKO, G., Leon, A.S., Jacobs, D.R., Jr., Foster, N., & Moy, J. Effect of exercise and/or weight loss on blood lipids in obese men on controlled diets. *Circulation*, 1982, **66** (Part 2), Il285.

STAMLER, J., Farinaro, E., Mojonnier, L.M., Hall, Y., Moss, D., & Stamler, R. Prevention and control of hypertension by nutritional hygienic means. *Journal of the American Medical Association*, 1980, **243**, 1819-1823.

SULLIVAN, L. Obesity, diabetes mellitus and physical activity-metabolic responses to physical training in adipose and muscle tissues. *Annals of Clinical Research*, 1982, **14**, 51-62.

TAYLOR, H.L., Buskirk, E.R., & Remington, R.D. Exercise in controlled trials of the prevention of coronary heart disease. *Federation Proceedings*, 1972, **32**, 1632-1627.

TAYLOR, H.L., Jacobs, D.R., Jr., Schucker, B., Knudsen, J., Leon, A.S., & DeBacker, G. A questionnaire for the assessment of leisure time physical activity. *Journal of Chronic Diseases*, 1978, **31**, 741-755.

THORLAND, W.G., & Gilliam, T.B. Comparisons of serum lipid between high and low active preadolescent males. *Medical Science in Sports and Exercise*, 1981, **13**, 316-321.

WEST, K.M. *Epidemiology of Diabetes and Its Vascular Lesions*. New York: Elsevier/North Holland Inc., 1978.

WHO Expert Committee. *Prevention of coronary heart disease*. Technical Report Series No. 678. Geneva: World Health Organization, 1982.

WILLETT, W., Hennekens, C.H., Castelli, W., Rosner, B., Evans, D., Taylor, J., & Kass, E.H. Effects of cigarette smoking on fasting triglycerides, total cholesterol, and HDL cholesterol in women. *American Heart Journal*, 1983, **105**, 417-421.

WILLETT, W., Hennekens, C.H., Siegel, A.J., Adner, M.M., & Castello, W.P. Alcohol consumption and high-density lipoprotein cholesterol in marathon runners. *New England Journal of Medicine*, 1980, **305**, 1159-1161.

WILLIAMS, P.T., Wood, P.D., Haskell, W.L., & Vranizan, K. The effects of running mileage and duration on plasma lipoprotein levels. *Journal of the American Medical Association*, 1982, **247**, 2674-2679.

WOOD, P.D., Haskell, W.L., Blair, S.H., Williams, P.T., Krauss, R.M., Lindgren, F.T., Albers, J.J., Ping, H., & Farquhar, J.W. Increased exercise level and plasma lipoprotein concentrations: A one-year, randomized, controlled study in sedentary, middle-aged men. *Metabolism*, 1983, **32**, 31-39.

WOOD, P.D., Haskell, W., Stern, M.P., Lewis, S., & Perry, C. Plasma lipopro-tein distributions in male and female runners. *Annals of the New York Academy of Science*, 1977, **301**, 748-763.

Exercise and Resting Blood Pressure

Charles M. Tipton
University of Iowa

To a physical educator, the words "exercise" and "health" are sacred and almost synonymous. It is evident from previous and current Academy proceedings that this imprinted viewpoint is somewhat justified, even though it must be recognized that not everyone who exercises will also be considered healthy.

Of the 11 topics scheduled for this symposium, this presentation is the only one concerned with a single measurement — a measurement that must be obtained and evaluated before most individuals will know whether their current health status is associated with higher, lower, or normal pressures. Unfortunately, between 10-20% of the individuals who are hypertensive are unaware of this fact (Levy, 1978). For purposes of this presentation, resting systolic and diastolic pressures that exceed 140/90 mmHg are considered to be hypertensive (Tipton, in press) even though some investigators use higher values (Thomas, Lee, Franks, & Paffenbarger, 1981) to indicate this condition. According to Frohlich (1979), "hypertension is a pandemic health problem that importantly affects the high vital statistics of cardiovascular morbidity and mortality worldwide" (p. 548). Because of the medical, psychological, and socioeconomic involvements, hypertension influences the lives of more than 60 million Americans in one form or another (Kaplan, 1978; Levy, 1978; Stamler, J., Farinaro, Mojonnier, Hall, Moss, & Stamler, R., 1978; Storer & Ruhling, 1981; Ward, 1981; Tipton, in press).

For classification purposes, there are two types of hypertension — primary and secondary — with 90% of the cases being primary (Tipton, in press). However, in 80-90% of the cases the mechanisms responsible for primary hypertension are unknown (Neufeld, 1974; Tipton, in press). Because the presence of elevated pressures does not reveal the origin for its elevation or the basis for its maintenance, recognizing and managing hypertension is almost as important as identifying the responsible mechanism. As indicated below, many factors have been associated with elevated pressures (Tipton, in press) including:

1. heredity;
2. fiber type distributions;
3. psychological changes;
4. autonomic nervous system imbalances;
5. central nervous system changes;
6. the toxemias of pregnancy;
7. hormonal elevations;
8. metabolic imbalances;
9. amount of body fat;
10. increased caloric intakes;
11. increased salt intakes;
12. magnitude of alcohol consumption;
13. degree of inactivity.

However, it is more important to emphasize the components of blood pressure than the myriad of conditions associated with its changes. According to Poiseuille's law (Folkow, 1982) blood pressure is the product of cardiac output and the vascular resistance to blood flow and can be expressed as:

Mean blood pressure = cardiac output × total peripheral resistance

$$\overline{X}BP = Q \times TPR$$

Therefore by altering cardiac output, total peripheral resistance, or both, one can manage blood pressure to within normotensive limits. This point must never be forgotten; hypertensive subjects who exhibit reductions in resting blood pressures will also experience reductions in the number of morbidity events and a delay in the mortality statistics even if normalization does not occur (Taguchi & Freis, 1975). Currently six distinct approaches (Tipton, in press) and numerous combinations are employed to lower resting pressures:

1. surgical interventions;
2. psychological counseling;
3. reductions in food intakes;
4. reductions in electrolyte intakes;
5. pharmacological interventions;
6. increases in physical activity.

Because most hypertensive individuals will not undergo surgery, the central issue is whether exercise training should be a specific or an adjunct approach in managing the condition.

The issue of exercise training and resting blood pressure was addressed 35 years ago by Schneider and Karpovich (1948), who concluded that increases, decreases, or no changes would occur. This concept continues and the topic remains controversial today.

Table 1

Impressions from Cross-sectional Studies

Normotensive populations

1. Studies involving approximately 25,000 individuals were examined.
2. Approximately 60% of the studies indicated that lower resting blood pressures were associated with active, athletic, or fit populations. In 30% of the comparisons, the athletic populations had higher resting pressures.
3. No discernible trend was apparent when the resting blood pressures of weight lifters or cyclists were examined.
4. The pressure differences associated with training ranged from 4-15 mmHg.

Hypertensive populations

1. Studies involving approximately 25,000 individuals were examined.
2. Lower resting pressures were generally associated with individuals considered to be active, fit, and lean.

To ascertain whether good grantsmanship is also good scholarship, this relationship was reexamined, as shown in Tables 1, 2, and 3. The trend from the cross-sectional studies (Table 1) was that individuals who were fit, lean, and/or physically active were also those who had lower pressures (5-15 mmHg). This trend was not immediately apparent from the longitudinal investigations (Table 2) because of the vast differences in designs and methods of data analysis. It was evident from the studies reviewed that: a) females were not included in most experimental designs; b) dynamic and endurance-type activities were most frequently studied; c) adequate control groups were noticeably absent; d) the methods of data analysis used were not suitable by 1980 standards; and e) little emphasis was given to whether cardiac output or total peripheral resistance had changed (Tipton, in press). Most of the studies did not monitor food and electrolyte intakes or psychological changes. On the other hand, they did measure body mass, a decrease of which was generally noted when positive results were noted (Tipton, in press).

Although numerous studies show that body weight decreases are also associated with decreases in resting blood pressures (Montoye, Metzner, Keller, Johnson, & Epstein, 1972; Stamler, R., Stamler, J., Riedlinger, Algera, & Roberts, 1978), there are many exceptions to this generalization (Horton, 1981). A few longitudinal studies in the end of the experimental period. Interestingly, most investigations that utilized direct arterial cannulations to measure pressure had post-training results that were either slightly elevated or similar to the pretraining values. On the other hand, the use of the stethoscope and the

Table 2

Impressions from Longitudinal Studies

Normotensive populations

1. Studies involving approximately 65 subjects were examined. More than 90% of these investigations had no nonexercising control groups.
2. When indirect methods were used to measure resting blood pressure, lower pressures were reported in approximately 70% of the comparisons.
3. When direct methods were used to measure resting blood pressure, lower pressures were reported in approximately 40% of the comparisons.
4. The pressure differences associated with training ranged from 4-21 mmHg.

Hypertensive populations

1. Studies involving approximately 360 subjects were examined. Approximately 50% of the investigations had nonexercising control groups. Only one study had both normotensive and hypertensive control groups.
2. When indirect methods were used, lower resting pressures were associated with training in approximately 75% of the studies.
3. When direct methods were used, lower resting pressures were associated with training in approximately 50% of the studies.
4. The older the subjects, the greater the benefit of training for resting blood pressure.
5. The pressure difference between the trained and nontrained groups ranged from 4-33 mmHg.

sphygmomanometer in training studies was usually identified with lower means. As noted in the cross-sectional studies, endurance training was associated with lower values, as systolic pressures generally changed by 8-15 mmHg and diastolic pressures by 4-10 mmHg. This trend was somewhat exaggerated with older subjects (> 60 yr), and if the initial systolic pressures were in the 120-130 mmHg range, minimal changes should be expected (Tipton, in press).

Although there is no overwhelming evidence to state unequivocally that endurance training alone will lower resting pressure in humans, there is sufficient evidence on the effects of exercise training on caloric consumption, body composition, hormonal levels, reflex actions, and autonomic nervous system functions to advocate exercise training for individuals with borderline and essential hypertension (Blomqvist & Saltin, 1983; Scheuer & Tipton, 1977; Tipton, Matthes, Marcus, Rowlett, & Woodson, in press; Tipton, in press). However, until food and electrolyte intakes, body composition changes, autonomic nervous system modifications, and personality alterations are carefully monitored in the same study it will be difficult to prove that exercise per se had lowered resting pressures.

One of the most interesting recent findings on possible mechanisms concerns the role of exercise training on resting insulin levels, with the end result being that less sodium is reabsorbed by the kidney tubules (Horton, 1981; Krotkiewski, Mandroukas, Sjostrom, Sullivan, Wetterqvist, & Bjorntorp, 1979; Sims, 1981). If correct, the changes in body mass and in fat content with exercise training are secondary to the changes at the kidney tubules for the reductions in resting pressures.

In 1980, 9% of all visits to physicians pertained to hypertension (National Center for Health Statistics, 1982). Medication was prescribed in 89% of these visits. Of the 10 drugs prescribed most for hypertension, six were diuretics and four blocked the actions of the sympathetic nervous system (Tipton, in press). Despite the plethora of anecdotal data, there is little experimental data demonstrating that exercise training will lower the dosage of antihypertensive medication humans need for normalization purposes. The recent animal results of Tipton et al. (1983) and the human studies of Hagberg, Goldberg, Ehsani, Heath, Delmez, and Harter (1983) suggest that this effect can occur; however, more investigations are needed to substantiate this. None of the cross-sectional and few of the longitudinal studies evaluated in Tables 1 and 2 examined changes in resting cardiac output or total peripheral resistance. Of the studies concerned with this, the results were far from consistent (Tipton, in press); however, they did suggest that training lowers the resting cardiac output and has a variable effect on total peripheral resistance.

Until more investigators include these measurements within the experimental design, speculation and controversy on the subject will continue. Not only have females been excluded from studies, but investigators have generally ignored the chronic effects of isometric or static exercises on resting blood pressure of normotensive and hypertensive groups (Tipton, in press). This is somewhat unexpected because cardiac risk patients are regularly advised not to perform these types of exercises.

Because of the reluctance of many, limited animal experimentation was done in the research laboratories affiliated with physical education departments until the 1960s. As listed in Table 3, the changes expected must be specific to the experimental condition being evaluated. As with the human studies, exercise training is seldom associated with higher resting values; thus this component of the Schneider and Karpovich statement (1948) listed earlier should be eliminated. While acknowledging its biased viewpoint, we believe resting blood pressure data from normotensive rats and primates (Scheuer & Tipton, 1977; Tipton et al., 1983; Tipton, in press) indicates that endurance training will usually be associated with lower resting pressures. However, the difference will seldom exceed 15 mmHg. When attempts were made to simulate conditions associated with borderline hypertension (DOCA injections, DOCA pellets, or renal artery clips), the results were variable, leaving one to select the trend that supports his or her beliefs (Table 1).

Table 3
Summary of Studies Using Animals

Normotensive rats

---

1. Studies involving more than 260 animals were examined.
2. Swimming and running exercise programs were used with male and female animals.
3. In more than 70% of the investigations, lower resting pressures were associated with the trained groups.
4. Positive and negative results were observed with both sexes and types of training programs.
5. The pressure differences between the trained and nontrained groups ranged from 5-18 mmHg.

DOCA-induced hypertensive rats

---

1. Studies involving more than 80 animals were examined.
2. Running was associated with lower resting pressures whereas both positive and negative results were obtained with swimming animals.

Renal hypertensive rats

---

1. Studies involving more than 40 animals were examined.
2. Running and swimming training programs were associated with either no marked differences or with higher resting pressures in the trained animals.
3. Mild training (40-60% $\dot{V}O_{2max}$) was also associated with increases in muscle enzymes and myocardial capillarization as well as higher pressures.

Genetically hypertensive rats (SHR)

---

1. Studies involving more than 400 rats were examined.
2. Swimming and running exercise programs were used with male and female animals.
3. In more than 75% of the studies, lower resting pressures were associated with the trained groups.
4. The influences of training was observed in both sexes and with both types of exercise programs.
5. The pressure differences between trained and nontrained groups ranged from 7-26 mmHg.

Salt-sensitive and resistant hypertensive rats

---

1. Studies involving more than 100 animals were examined.
2. Swimming and running programs were used with female animals.
3. Lower resting blood pressures were always observed with the trained rats that were salt-sensitive. This effect was also observed in the majority of studies with the trained rats that were salt-resistant.
4. The pressure differences between the trained and nontrained groups ranged from 7-55 mmHg.

Table 3 (Cont.)

Stroke-prone hypertensive rats

1. One study with more than 75 animals was examined.
2. Voluntary exercise in activity wheels was associated with lower resting pressures during the early stages of training and with higher pressures as the program continued.
3. The pressure differences between the trained and nontrained male animals ranged from 18-22 mmHg.

Non-human primates

1. One study involving 10 animals was examined.
2. A running program was used for 20 weeks.
3. At the end of the experiment, the trained animals had a resting pressure value that was 10 mmHg lower than the controls.

Unlike investigators studying humans, most scientists using animals, particularly rats, have failed to quantify the oxygen requirements of the training program (Bedford et al., 1979). While this may not be a serious issue with normotensive animals, it is clearly a major consideration with animal models for disease, especially for hypertension. As recently documented by Tipton and associates (1983), exercise training by genetically hypertensive rats (SHR) in excess of 75% $\dot{V}O_{2max}$ results in higher resting blood pressures. However, endurance training by SHR groups at 40-60% of their $\dot{V}O_{2max}$ is associated with lower resting pressures. This effect is sufficiently consistent with younger and older rats to suggest that the concept be considered for hypertensive humans (Tipton et al., 1983; Tipton, in press). At the moment, this pressure effect is explained by Reis' central imbalance theory which states that hypertension occurs from the inability of the CNS to effectively integrate autonomic influences originating from the external environment (Tipton, in press). Therefore, without quantifying the exercise programs used for animals, investigators will confuse rather than advance the role of exercise training in diseased models.

In hypertension research, the different animal models for the disease have been instrumental in gaining meaningful insights on responsible mechanisms and on management principles (Frohlich & Trippodo, 1981; McGiff & Quilley, 1981). This is particularly true with the use of pharmacological agents to reduce resting pressures. For several years we have tried to determine whether exercise training and reduced dosages of antihypertensive medication will normalize resting blood pressure in hypertensive rats. After several years of effort, we found that in males, moderate exercise (40-60% $\dot{V}O_{2max}$) with medication equal to 85% of the required value would normalize resting pressures in the trained but not in the nontrained (Tipton et al., 1983). Why a sex difference occurred is unknown at this time.

From the in vitro and in vivo animal studies we have reviewed or performed, it appears that exercise training lowers resting blood pressure because of a combination of effects. These include a reduced sympathetic nerve traffic to the arterioles, a change in the intrinsic tone of vascular smooth muscle, an increased vascular lumen, a change in baroreflexes, a decrease in circulating insulin and/or a reduction in heart rate (Tipton, in press). These possibilities help to explain our results and those of Shephard, Kuehne, Kenno, Durstine, Balon, & Rapp (1982), who reported training effects with hypertensive rats that were sensitive to the presence of salt. Currently we are extending our studies to hypertensive and stroke-prone rats while attempting to perfect isometric training protocols for them. Although the animal data are limited (Gleeson, Mullin, & Baldwin, 1983), we feel that a decrease in resting blood pressure is due more to a decrease in cardiac output than to a decrease in total peripheral resistance.

In summary, the evidence on the relationship between blood pressure and endurance training is extensive but not conclusive. Seldom will exercise training result in higher resting pressures, although the possibility is higher when using direct methods of assessment. Using indirect methods and older subjects will generally be associated with lower values. Despite our skepticism concerning the nature of the existing data, we believe there is sufficient justification to advocate exercise training as a specific approach for hypertensive populations, especially those with borderline pressures. In most situations the training benefit will seldom exceed 15 mmHg; thus adjunct approaches must always be considered. We also believe the current emphasis on metabolic changes should be shifted to examine how alterations in insulin concentrations and in tissue sensitivities will alter sodium reabsorption levels. Additional areas requiring extra attention are sex differences, role of isometric exercises, medication levels, and responsible mechanisms.

Studies on the role of exercise training in hypertension must include animals, as the increased availability of genetic and environmental animal models provide the experimental means to vigorously control the factors responsible for changes in pressure. However, science will not be served if investigators fail to quantify the exercise schedules being advocated. Finally, members of the Academy or the profession of physical education must never again minimize the importance of animal research in understanding the health problems affecting humans.

REFERENCES

BEDFORD, T.G., Tipton, C.M., Wilson, N.C., Oppliger, R.A., & Gisolfi, C.V. Maximum oxygen consumption of rats and its changes with various experimental procedures. *Journal of Applied Physiology*, 1979, **47**, 1278-1283.

BLOMQVIST, C.G., & Saltin, B. Cardiovascular adaptations to physical training. *Annual Review of Physiology*, 1983, **45**, 169-189.

FOLKOW, B. Physiological aspects of primary hypertension. *Physiological Reviews*, 1982, **62**, 347-503.

FROHLICH, E.D. Special report: Review of the WHO expert committee report on arterial hypertension. *Hypertension*, 1979, **1**, 547-548.

FROHLICH, E.D., & Trippodo, N.C. Response to "The rat with spontaneous genetic hypertension is not a suitable model of human essential hypertension." *Circulation Research*, 1981, **48**, 464.

GLEESON, T.T., Mullin, W.J., & Baldwin, K.M. Cardiovascular responses to treadmill exercise in rats: Effects of training. *Journal of Applied Physiology: Respiratory, Environmental and Exercise Physiology*, 1983, **54**, 789-793.

HAGBERG, J.M., Goldberg, A.P., Ehsani, A.A., Heath, G.W., Delmez, J.D., & Harter, H.R. Exercise training improves hypertension in hemodialysis patients. *American Journal of Nephrology*, 1983, **3**, 209-212.

HORTON, E.S. The role of exercise in the treatment of hypertension in obesity. *International Journal of Obesity*, 1981, **5**, 165-171.

KAPLAN, N.M. *Clinical hypertension*. Baltimore: Williams & Wilkins, 1978.

KROTKIEWSKI, M., Mandroukas, K., Sjostrom, L., Sullivan, L., Wetterqvist, H., & Bjorntorp, P. Effect of long-term physical training on body fat, metabolism, and blood pressure in obesity. *Metabolism*, 1979, **28**, 650-658.

LEVY, R.I. Progress in prevention of cardiovascular disease. *Preventive Medicine*, 1978, **7**, 464-475.

McGIFF, J.C., & Quilley, C.P. Controversies in cardiovascular research. The rat with spontaneous genetic hypertension is not a suitable model of human essential hypertension. *Circulation Research*, 1981, **48**, 455-463.

MONTOYE, H.J., Metzner, H.L., Keller, J.B., Johnson, B.C., & Epstein, F.H. Habitual physical activity and blood pressure. *Medicine and Science in Sports*, 1972, **4**, 175-181.

NATIONAL Center for Health Statistics. Drug utilization in office practice by age and sex of the patient. *Advance Data* (HRA), 1982, **3**, 1-12.

NATIONAL Center for Health Statistics. Medication therapy in office visits for hypertension. *Advance Data* (HRA), 1982, **2**, 1-12.

NEUFELD, H.N. Precursors of coronary arteriosclerosis in the pediatric and young adult age groups. *Modern Concepts of Cardiovascular Disease*, 1974, **43**, 93-97.

SCHEUER, J.T., & Tipton, C.M. Cardiovascular adaptations to physical training. *Annual Review of Physiology*, 1977, **39**, 221-251.

SCHNEIDER, E.C., & Karpovich, P.V. *Physiology of muscular activity.* Philadelphia: W.B. Saunders, 1948.

SHEPHARD, R.E., Kuehne, M.L., Kenno, K.A., Durstine, J.L., Balon, T.W., & Rapp, J.R. Attenuation of blood pressure increases in Dahl salt-sensitive rats by exercise. *Journal of Applied Physiology: Respiratory, Environmental and Exercise Physiology*, 1982, **42**, 1608-1613.

SIMS, E.A.H. Mechanisms of hypertension in the syndrome of obesity. *International Journal of Obesity*, 1981, **5**, 9-18.

STAMLER, R., Stamler, J., Riedlinger, W.F., Algera, G., & Roberts, R.H. Weight and blood pressure. Findings in hypertension screenings of 1 million Americans. *Journal of the American Medical Association*, 1978, **240**, 1607-1612.

STAMLER, J., Farinaro, E., Mojonnier, L.M., Hall, Y., Moss, D., & Stamler, R. Prevention and control of hypertension by nutritional-hygienic means. *Journal of the American Medical Association*, 1980, **234**, 1819-1823.

STORER, T.W., & Ruhling, R.O. Essential hypertension and exercise. *Physician and Sportsmedicine*, 1981, **9**, 59-69.

TAGUCHI, J., & Freis, E.D. Partial versus complete control of blood pressure in the prevention of hypertensive complications. *Circulation Research*, 1975, **36**, 1257-1260.

THOMAS, G.S., Lee, P.R., Franks, T., & Paffenbarger, R.S. *Exercise and health*. Cambridge, MA: Oelgeschlager, Gunn, & Hain, 1981.

TIPTON, C.M. Exercise, training and hypertension. *Exercise Sport Science Reviews*, in press.

TIPTON, C.M., Matthes, R.D., Callahan, A., Tcheng, T.K., & Lais, L.T. The role of chronic exercise on resting blood pressure of normotensive and hypertensive rats. *Medicine and Science in Sports*, 1977, **9**, 168-177.

TIPTON, C.M., Matthes, R.D., Marcus, K.D., Rowlett, K.A., & Leininger, J.R. Influence of exercise intensity, age, and medication on resting systolic blood pressure of SHR populations. *Journal of Applied Physiology: Respiratory, Environmental and Exercise Physiology*, 1983, **55**, 1305-1310.

WARD, G.W. An overview of the National High Blood Pressure Educational Program in the United States. In T. Phillips & A. Distler (Eds.), *Hypertension: Mechanisms and Management*. Berlin: Springer-Verlag, 1980.

Recent Progress in Understanding Obesity

Lawrence B. Oscai
University of Illinois at Chicago

About 15 years ago, we began examining the role of exercise in weight control (Oscai & Williams, 1968). Initially our efforts focused on correcting mild and moderate obesity, and later, severe obesity. Due to lack of success in treating severe obesity in humans, the direction of our work shifted from correcting it to preventing it. To prevent severe obesity, it was necessary to first identify its contributing factors. In the course of ongoing work, evidence has shown that the neonatal feeding experience can produce a wide range in the total-body content of fat. More important, dietary fat may play a dominant role in developing severe obesity in the rat. This report presents a brief summary of our progress in understanding obesity.

TREATMENT OF OBESITY IN HUMANS

The Framingham Heart Disease study gives us data on normal fluctuations in body weight that occurred in the general population over a period of 18 years (Gordon & Kannel, 1973). In the study, body weight was found to fluctuate about 21 pounds (9.6 kg), but this chiefly reflected short-term fluctuations. Persistent changes occurred very slowly, and weight at one age was closely related to weight later in life for most people. Exercise appears effective in correcting the increases in body weight associated with the short-term fluctuations. For example, 10 mildly overweight males (5 runners and 5 controls) from 35 to 46 years of age were matched for weight and asked to participate in an endurance training program (Oscai & Williams, 1968). They ran three times per

This work was supported by the United States Public Health Service Research Grant AM-17357.

week for 16 weeks. During each session they ran at least 30 minutes and covered at least three miles. The results showed that with exercise, body weight decreased an average of 4.5 kg. The weight loss primarily resulted from a loss of body fat. While it was possible to correct mild obesity, it was not possible to correct severe obesity (200-500 lbs for males) with exercise alone.

These results did not surprise us because other investigators have repeatedly failed in trying to treat obesity, regardless of the method used (Stunkard & McLaren-Hume, 1959). Generally, it is possible to decrease body weight in grossly overweight individuals but it is nearly impossible to maintain that decrease over a number of years. Hence obesity, particularly the severe form, is now considered by some to be an incurable disorder (Mann, 1974). Because of the difficulties in treating severe obesity, the focus of our research shifted from correction to a search for factors that cause severe obesity.

NEONATAL FEEDING EXPERIENCE
AND INCREASED BODY FAT STORES

The long-term effects of the neonatal feeding experience are associated with a permanently fixed appetite and body weight at higher-than-normal or lower-than-normal levels (Oscai & McGarr, 1978). Apparently the mechanisms regulating voluntary food intake are fixed, to some extent, by the amount of food consumed in the first 21 days of life in the rat. As adults, the contribution of the neonatal feeding experience to increased body fat stores can be seen from two comparisons (Oscai, 1982). First, of the rats eating a low-fat diet of Purina chow, those programed for a high caloric intake had carcasses averaging 88 g more fat than those programed for a low caloric intake. Of interest, rats eating the low-fat diet never did become severely obese as adults; the results showed that animals programed for a high caloric intake remained moderately obese (29% body fat), whereas those programed for a low caloric intake remained lean (18% body fat). Second, of the rats eating a fat-rich diet (42% of calories from fat), those programed for a high caloric intake had carcasses averaging 202 g more fat than those programed for a low caloric intake.

In contrast to the low-fat diet, both groups eating the fat-rich diet became severely obese (59-61% body fat). Thus, while the neonatal feeding experience has been shown to produce a wide range in body fatness, dietary fat has the power to override the neonatal feeding experience. Moreover, dietary fat appears to be a dominant factor in developing severe obesity.

DIETARY FAT AS A CENTRAL FACTOR
IN DEVELOPING SEVERE OBESITY

Nearly 55 years ago, Reed, Yamaguchi, Anderson, and Mendel (1930) reported that fat-rich diets accelerate the rate of weight gain and body fat content in rats. Since then numerous reports have supported this notion in animals (Barboriak, Krehl, Cowgill, & Whedon, 1958; Barki, Collins, Elvehjem, & Hart, 1950; Deuel, Meserve, Straub, Hendrick, & Scheer, 1947; Dryden, Foley, Gleis, & Hartman, 1956; Fenton & Carr, 1951; Forbes, Swift, Elliott, & James, 1946; Haldi, Giddings, & Wynn, 1942; Hoagland & Snider, 1940; Mickelsen, Takahashi, & Craig, 1955; Peckham, Entenman, & Carroll, 1962; Schemmel, Mickelsen, & Tolgay, 1969; Thomasson, 1955). One way in which dietary fat contributes to a faster rate of weight gain and severe obesity is that it causes animals to overeat, thus increasing the total number of calories consumed (Maller, 1964; Schemmel, Mickelsen, & Gill, 1970; Schemmel, Mickelsen, & Fisher, 1973; Oscai, 1982). For example, in a previous study (Oscai, 1982) the long-term ingestion of a fat-rich diet caused hyperphagia such that the appetites of male rats were highly stimulated between 29 and 58 weeks of age. As adults, these animals became severely obese; their carcasses averaged 61% fat.

In contrast to overeating, evidence now shows that rats consuming a fat-rich diet can become severely obese without overeating (Oscai & Brown, submitted). This evidence comes from the observation that voluntary food intake averaged 36,113 ± 410 calories/rat per 60 weeks for those eating a high-fat diet (42% of calories from fat) compared to a value of 36,125 ± 590 calories/rat per 60 weeks for those eating a diet of Purina chow. In spite of a similar caloric intake, carcass fat averaged 51 ± 1% (severe obesity) for rats eating the fat-rich diet but only 30 ± 1% body fat (moderate obesity) for those eating the low-fat diet of Purina chow. These results clearly demonstrate that severe obesity can develop without overeating, provided the animals eat a fat-rich diet.

There is support for the concept of obesity without overeating. About 36 years ago, Lundbaek and Stevenson (1947) fed weight-stable female rats of a Sprague-Dawley strain either a fat-rich or carbohydrate-rich diet for 16 weeks. They reported that the average caloric intake was 39 calories per day on the carbohydrate diet and 41 calories per day on the fat diet. In spite of this, the rats on the fat diet gained an average of 0.6 g per day, while those on the carbohydrate diet kept their weight practically unchanged. In a more recent study, Schemmel et al. (1970) reported that after 20 weeks of fat feeding, several different strains of rats increased their body fat stores without overeating. Fat feeding caused an approximate 2.8-fold increase in the total-body content of fat without any increase in the total number of calories consumed in Hoppert (males), Wistar-Lewis (females), and Gray (females) compared with their controls of the same sex and strain eating a low-fat grain diet. Other investigators have noted a faster rate of weight gain in the absence of overeating in rats (Herberg, Döppen, Major, & Gries, 1974; Jen, Greenwood, & Brasel, 1981; Lemonnier, 1972) and in hamsters (Wade, 1982) consuming a fat-rich diet.

Taken together, the above results are strong evidence that, in a completely unpredictable fashion, either overeating or non-overeating will occur in a given group of rats eating a fat-rich diet. We do not yet understand why dietary fat should cause overeating in some cases but not in others. Obviously, the focus of future work will be to determine the mechanisms that "turn on" appetite stimulation or keep it "turned off" in animals eating a fat-rich diet. In view of these results, the belief that rats typically overeat when given a fat-rich diet needs to be reexamined (Wade, 1982; 1983).

OTHER FACTORS THOUGHT TO
PLAY A ROLE IN OBESITY

A number of factors are thought to be involved in the development of obesity. Among others, they include brown adipose tissue abnormalities (Rothwell & Stock, 1979; Himms-Hagen, 1979), the size of the adipocyte (Faust, Johnson, & Hirsch, 1977), stress, dietary sugar (Kanarek & Hirsch, 1977), genetics, endocrine disorders, lack of exercise, neonatal feeding experience, and dietary fat. Aside from exercise, dietary fat, and the neonatal feeding experience, dietary sugar is of particular interest since evidence shows that sucrose feeding can increase body fat stores (Kanarek & Hirsch, 1977). However, the actual contribution of dietary sugar in developing severe obesity is uncertain because the long-term, baseline studies needed to document its contribution to the grossly overweight condition have never been carried out. As it now stands, body weight of animals fed sucrose has never been shown to exceed 650 g. Obviously, the focus of future work will be to determine dietary sugar's precise contribution to obesity.

SUMMARY

In recent years, the problem of concern has been to identify factors that contribute to severe obesity. This is because severe obesity is generally considered incurable when employing conventional treatment methods such as exercise, diet, and/or drugs. As a first step in prevention, our efforts have centered on the neonatal feeding experience and dietary fat. An attractive feature of our work thus far is that it is possible to produce body fatness in adult rats ranging from the lean condition (18% body fat) to the severely obese condition (61% body fat). The severe form of obesity can be produced by the long-term ingestion of dietary fat, and this condition can develop with or without overeating. On the basis of these results, it is our working hypothesis that dietary fat plays a major regulatory role in the development of severe obesity. In relation to exercise, it is now possible to examine the role of physical activity in severe obesity because a model for the grossly overweight condition has been developed. Our animal model has body fat percentages within the range of many obese individuals. Finally, the fat composition of the animal diet is similar to the one used by a majority of people in the United States where obesity is a problem.

REFERENCES

BARBORIAK, J.J., Krehl, W.A., Cowgill, G.R., & Whedon, A.D. Influence of high-fat diets on growth and development of obesity in the albino rat. *Journal of Nutrition*, 1958, **64**, 241-249.

BARKI, V.H., Collins, R.A., Elvehjem, C.A., & Hart, E.B. The importance of the dietary level of fats on their nutritional evaluation. *Journal of Nutrition*, 1950, **40**, 383-392.

DEUEL, H.J., Jr., Meserve, E.R., Straub, E., Hendrick, C., & Scheer, B.T. The effect of fat level of the diet on general nutrition. I. Growth, reproduction and physical capacity of rats receiving diets containing various levels of cottonseed oil or margarine fat ad libitum. *Journal of Nutrition*, 1947, **33**, 569-582.

DRYDEN, L.P., Foley, J.B., Gleis, P.F., & Hartman, A.M. Experiments on the comparative nutritive value of butter and vegetable fats. *Journal of Nutrition*, 1956, **58**, 189-201.

FAUST, I.M., Johnson, P.R., & Hirsch, J. Surgical removal of adipose tissue alters feeding behavior and the development of obesity in rats. *Science*, 1977, **197**, 393-396.

FENTON, P.F., & Carr, C.J. The nutrition of the mouse. XI. Response of four strains to diets differing in fat content. *Journal of Nutrition*, 1951, **45**, 225-233.

FORBES, E.B., Swift, R.W., Elliott, R.F., & James, W.H. Relation of fat to economy of food utilization. *Journal of Nutrition*, 1946, **31**, 203-212.

GORDON, T., & Kannel, W.B. The effects of overweight on cardiovascular diseases. *Geriatrics*, 1973, **28**, 80-88.

HALDI, J., Giddings, G., & Wynn, W. Dietary control of the water content of the skin of the albino rat. *American Journal of Physiology*, 1942, **135**, 392-397.

HERBERG, L., Döppen, W., Major, E., & Gries, F.A. Dietary-induced hypertrophic-hyperplastic obesity in mice. *Journal of Lipid Research*, 1974, **15**, 580-585.

HIMMS-HAGEN, J. Obesity may be due to a malfunctioning of brown fat. *Canadian Medical Association Journal*, 1979, **121**, 1361-1364.

HOAGLAND, R., & Snider, G.G. Nutritive properties of certain animal and vegetable fats. *U.S. Department of Agriculture Technical Bulletin no. 725*. 1940, pp. 1-12.

JEN, K-L.C., Greenwood, M.R.C., & Brasel, J.A. Sex differences in the effects of high-fat feeding on behavior and carcass composition. *Physiology and Behavior*, 1981, **27**, 161-166.

KANAREK, R.B., & Hirsch, E. Dietary-induced overeating in experimental animals. *Federation Proceedings*, 1977, **36**, 154-158.

LEMONNIER, D. Effect of age, sex, and site on the cellularity of the adipose tissue in mice and rats rendered obese by a high-fat diet. *Journal of Clinical Investigation*, 1972, **51**, 2907-2915.

LUNDBAEK, K., & Stevenson, J.A.F. Reduced carbohydrate intake after fat feeding in normal rats and rats with hypothalamic hyperphagia. *American Journal of Physiology*, 1947, **151**, 530-537.

MALLER, O. The effect of hypothalamic and dietary obesity on taste preference in rats. *Life Sciences*, 1964, **3**, 1281-1291.

MANN, G.V. The influence of obesity on health. *New England Journal of Medicine*, 1974, **291**, 176-232.

MICKELSEN, O., Takahashi, S., & Craig, C. Experimental obesity. I. Production of obesity in rats by feeding high-fat diets. *Journal of Nutrition*, 1955, **57**, 541-554.

OSCAI, L.B. Dietary-induced severe obesity: A rat model. *American Journal of Physiology: Regulatory Integrative and Comparative Physiology*, 1982, **242**, R212-R215.

OSCAI, L.B., & Brown, M.M. Severe obesity without overeating in rats. (Submitted for publication.)

OSCAI, L.B., & McGarr, J.A. Evidence that the amount of food consumed in early life fixes appetite in the rat. *American Journal of Physiology: Regulatory Integrative and Comparative Physiology*, 1978, **235**, R141-R144.

OSCAI, L.B., & Williams, B.T. Effect of exercise on overweight middle-aged males. *Journal of American Geriatrics Society*, 1968, **16**, 794-797.

PECKHAM, S.C., Entenman, C., & Carroll, H.W. The influence of a hypercaloric diet on gross body and adipose tissue composition in the rat. *Journal of Nutrition*, 1962, **77**, 187-197.

REED, L.L., Yamaguchi, F., Anderson, W.E., & Mendel, L.B. Factors influencing the distribution and character of adipose tissue in the rat. *The Journal of Biological Chemistry*, 1930, **87**, 147-155.

ROTHWELL, N.J., & Stock, M.J. A role for brown adipose tissue in diet-induced thermogenesis. *Nature*, 1979, **281**, 31-35.

SCHEMMEL, R., Mickelsen, O., & Fisher, L. Body composition and fat depot weights of rats as influenced by ration fed dams during lactation and that fed rats after weaning. *Journal of Nutrition*, 1973, **103**, 477-487.

SCHEMMEL, R., Mickelsen, O., & Gill, J.L. Dietary obesity in rats: Body weight and body fat accretion in seven strains of rats. *Journal of Nutrition*, 1970, **100**, 1041-1048.

SCHEMMEL, R., Mickelsen, O., & Tolgay, Z. Dietary obesity in rats: Influence of diet, weight, and sex on body composition. *The American Journal of Physiology*, 1969, **216**, 373-379.

STUNKARD, A., & McLaren-Hume, M. The results of treatment for obesity. A review of the literature and report of a series. *American Medical Association Archives of Internal Medicine*, 1959, **103**, 79-85.

THOMASSON, H.J. The biological value of oils and fats. I. Growth and food intake on feeding with natural oils and fats. *Journal of Nutrition*, 1955, **56**, 455-468.

WADE, G.N. Obesity without overeating in golden hamsters. *Physiology and Behavior*, 1982, **29**, 701-707.

WADE, G.N. Dietary obesity in golden hamsters: Reversibility and effects on sex and photoperiod. *Physiology and Behavior*, 1983, **30**, 131-137.

Exercise and Arthropathy

Bruno Balke
Sportsmedicine & Fitness Institute, The Aspen Club

Arthropathy is a collective term for pathological changes in joints, either of inflammatory or degenerative nature. Generally, all the joint diseases are grouped under the term "arthritis." Probably about 10% of the world's population suffer more or less severely from the disease. In the United States alone, about 20 million people are afflicted severely enough to seek medical attention. It is commonly believed that arthritis sufferers must settle down to a life of inactivity to avoid the often excruciating pain. However, we have learned that avoidance of movements creates a vicious cycle, leading to even more problems.

FORMS OF ARTHROPATHY

Arthritis, as denoted in medical language by the ending "itis," is an inflammatory process. I learned about 50 years ago in medical school that in any inflammatory disease, physical activity is either contraindicated or at least prescribed with restrictions. Actually that rule has changed very little since then.

Professor von Domarus (1935), one of my former teachers in medical school, differentiated in his textbook of internal medicine between the following forms of joint disease:

1. Metabolic disorders, such as in arthritis urica or gout, a disease resulting from a disturbance of uric acid metabolism; it is characterized by an excess of uric acid in the blood and deposits of uric acid salts in joints and tendons;

2. Inflammatory processes in a variety of joints, as in rheumatic arthritis, or in specific infectious arthritis (e.g., caused by gonococci, staphylococci, mycobacteria, or viruses);

3. Degenerative disease of joint cartilage and adjacent bone structure that has primarily nothing to do with any form of inflammation; this chronic disease, developing over a long period of
time, is termed osteoarthrosis.

Thus, under the popular term arthritis are many joint afflictions
whose fundamental cause for many forms is still not well known. In true
arthritis, the synovia (i.e., the inner lining of the joint capsule) is inflamed, resulting in the typical symptoms of swelling, increased
temperature, reddened skin around the joint area, and pain. In the acute
process the joint space usually fills with fluid and therefore becomes
enlarged. Eventually, however, the inflammation of the periarticular
tissue causes the capsule to shrink, leading to ankylosis—a pathological
joining of fibrous parts within the joint. In that case the articular space
might no longer exist. Joints are then often fixed in a flexed position.

In contrast, osteoarthrosis is a pathological process of a noninflam-
matory basis. Most often, cartilage and bone structures degenerate only
in major joints, especially the weight-bearing joints of knees and hips.
The shoulders are less often afflicted. Although the joint cavity remains
essentially intact, there is a destruction of the articular surface with an
exuberant growth of cartilage and bony masses around the articular
edges (Bluestone, 1982). The new bony mass is of poor quality, sometimes resulting in the formation of relatively large bony cysts. Such cysts
can severely restrict the joint's mobility. Also, intraarticular folds of the
synovial membrane may become ossified, giving cause to floating cor-
puscles within the joint and leading to more damage of the joint surface.

EXERCISE IN ACUTE ARTHRITIS

An acutely inflamed joint will not benefit from active movements. However, during recent years the approach to exercise treatment has changed
for many diseases. Early ambulation has been found not only safe but
even desirable for preventing ill effects of prolonged bed rest. In acute
arthritis, early *passive* movements of the afflicted joints have been found
useful to keep the range of motion intact as far as possible (Bardwick,
1982; Crabbe & Cilento, 1980; Krewer & Edgar, 1981; Schutt, 1977). In
order to prevent severe muscle atrophy that invariably follows even
short-term immobilization of a joint, the adjacent muscle groups must be
exercised by isometric contractions. The strength of the extensor muscles
especially must be maintained in order to compensate for the dominance
of the flexor groups. Otherwise the joint may eventually become fixed in
a flexed position. Since the neuromuscular mechanism for an isometric
contraction is sometimes inhibited by the anticipated pain in the joint, it
is usually helpful to begin the required isometric contraction on the

nonafflicted limb. That will facilitate the proper nerve impulses to the appropriate muscles on the diseased side. With such a type of isometric exercise, the joint is not moved and pain should therefore be minimal.

Whenever there is a remission from acute arthritis, even if a slight chronic disability exists, exercise treatment changes from passive to more active movements of the joint and emphasizes stretching of the flexor and strengthening of the extensor muscles. Heating pads and massage of the proximal muscle groups should support the exercise treatment. For general conditioning, swimming and resistance movements in comfortably warm water are recommended for any form of chronic arthritis. If complete remission from rheumatic or infectious arthritis occurs with only minimal damage to intraarticular spaces, any sport or physical activity should be permissible as long as it can be performed enjoyably. Since physical inactivity seems to be a cause of osteoporosis, such renewed physical activity is important for preserving bone mass (Hancock, Asiedu-Offei, Atkinson, Reed, & Wright, 1978).

PERIARTICULAR PAIN

People often complain about arthritic pain without really suffering from true inflammatory or degenerative joint disease. The periarticular tissue of ligaments, tendons, and muscles is closely connected to the joint capsule and to the periost of the adjacent bones. Overuse of muscles often results in a sort of hardening or spasm-like contraction of parts in the muscle belly. Consequently, the stiffening of the entire muscle causes an excessive continuous pull of its tendon at the place of insertion, resulting in a painful periostitis and tendinitis in the area of attachment. The "tennis elbow" and the "Achilles tendinitis" are two examples. Likewise, disturbing pain in either one or both knees develops sometimes on long stretches of walking downhill, an activity that causes great strain on the m. quadriceps femoris. Stretching of the spastic muscles and a deep kneading massage are applied to relieve the pain. Thus, in such cases of "pseudo-arthritis" the localization and appropriate treatment of the "culprit" among the muscles restores pain-free joint function.

OSTEOARTHROSIS: ETIOLOGY AND PATHOLOGY

Joints are composed of articular cartilage laid down over bone ends and a synovial membrane that produces the synovial fluid for ideal lubrication. Rich vascular and lymphatic systems in the joint capsule facilitate the movement of material into and out of the joint.

Bone and cartilage must resist the forces of compression, bending, and tension. The principal matrix of the elastic cartilage are macro-molecules of collagen and of the mucopolysacharide proteoglycan. Dense layers of collagen on the articular surface prevent the leakage of proteoglycan from the deeper layers of the cartilage matrix into the articular space. They also prevent harmful enzymes in the synovial fluid from entering the deeper cartilage substance (Bullough, 1979). In ongoing catalytic activity, the proteoglycan is the component most readily lost. But it is also readily replaced by actions of the chondrocyte cells in the basic layers of the cartilage. These cells produce proteoglycan, maintaining a balance between its degradation and synthesis (Dingle, 1978).

When proteoglycan degeneration exceeds its regeneration by the chondrocytes, superficial layers of collagen fibers flake off and crevices form on the surface (Bernhard, 1982), allowing proteoglycan to leak out into the joint cavity. The same can happen if the cartilage is damaged by direct trauma. Another reason for the loss of cartilage can be a diminished synthesis of proteoglycan, resulting from a lack of mechanical stress that is needed for the stimulation of its production. In any case, when breakdown occurs faster than repair, the joint degenerates (Bullough, 1979).

In surveying the literature, one encounters a number of conflicting statements about the genesis of osteoarthrosis. According to some researchers, it is simply a degenerative process of aging (Freeman, 1979), while others say that getting older has primarily nothing to do with it. There is no doubt, however, that the incidence rate increases with age (Bernhard, 1982).

The theory of microtrauma to the joint surface in the etiology of osteoarthrosis is also not generally accepted. Conflicting evidence is presented by those who tried to establish the role of physical activity and sports as a contributing factor in the development of arthropathy. According to Murray and Duncan (1971), a tilt deformity between the head and neck of the femur, a consequence of injury to the epiphyseal plate in youth, precipitates degenerative joint changes. They X-rayed the hips of 251 boys between 17 and 21 years of age who participated in various forms of sports. Those participating in jumping events (high and broad jump, pole vaulting, and hurdling) had by far the highest incidence of tilt deformity. Next were gymnasts and cross-country runners. The authors concluded that degenerative disease of the hip has a distribution corresponding to the degree of interest and participation in competitive athletic activities. A similar view was expressed by a South African doctor who stated that "strenuous exercise, marathon running and jogging in particular, constitute aberrant behaviour, analogous to drug addiction. It most likely leads to chronic orthopedic disability and is an important factor in explaining the high incidence of coronary artery disease in South Africa" (Grant-Whyte, 1980).

Of course, there is no scientific evidence for such a statement (Noakes, 1981). Puranen, Ala-Ketola, Peltokallio, and Saarela (1975) studied a group of 74 former elite runners and compared them to 115 hospital patients who were X-rayed for other reasons than hip complaints. Of the runners, only one had severe and two others had moderate changes indicative of osteoarthrosis (a total of 4%). In the control group they found two severe and eight moderate cases, a total of 8.7%. Playing soccer appears to present a higher risk: A study by Klunder, Rud, and Hansen (1980) revealed a significantly greater prevalence of arthrosis among retired soccer players, compared with controls. The hip was more frequently affected than the knee, contrary to what one would assume.

In the *Encyclopedia of Sport Sciences and Medicine*, articles by Lowman (1971) pointed out that coaching an athlete without attending to correctable faults in his or her body mechanics may promote an early "wear and tear arthritis." Performance, he says, is contingent on the efficacy in alignment of body structures. Structural deviations and bad biomechanics from faults in posture, growth, and development are a definite factor in later functional ailments. We know that an abnormal arch of the foot, uneven leg length, deviations from the normal curvature of the spine, or slight pelvic abnormalities can, in the long run, lead to musculoskeletal trauma affecting joint function.

In addition, allergic or toxic reactions to foods, hormonal disturbances, vitamin deficiencies, and also vasoconstricting effects of smoking may have some impact on the development of osteoarthrosis. Most probably a combination of various noxious influences contributes to the genesis of this crippling disease.

TREATMENT OF OSTEOARTHROSIS

Prevention of osteoarthrosis is practically impossible because the symptoms in its initial stages of development are usually not sufficiently characteristic to raise much suspicion. An athletically inclined person occasionally experiences slight injuries of the musculoskeletal system that are not seriously harmful and therefore do not cause much concern. It so happens that the healthy and fit body has a great capacity to compensate somehow for functional shortcomings. Our present knowledge does not enable us to predict individual susceptibility to any of the hundred forms of arthropathy. Once the disease has progressed to a state of persistent discomfort and minor physical handicap, one can only attempt to delay further progress of the disease with prophylactic measures. The prophylaxis may include dietary measures (Fredericks, 1981), physical therapy (Bardwick, 1982; Neff, 1978), exercise (Crabbe & Cilento, 1980;

Krewer & Edgar, 1981; Miller & LeLieuvre, 1982; Schutt, 1977) and medication.

Medication

No drug has yet been found that would control tissue catabolism in the cartilage matrix of patients with osteoarthrosis. The most useful agent in diminishing inflammation and reducing tissue catabolism has been the steroids. But the side effects of prolonged Cortisol application are so severe that they limit their clinical usefulness (Dingle, 1978). Painkillers are only temporarily effective but allow one to maintain a sufficient amount of physical activity. Pertinent drugs are not a cure, nor are they well tolerated by many people for a prolonged time.

Nutrition

The efficiency of nutrition in the prevention or prophylaxis of arthropathy depends upon whom one wants to believe: the physician who says that no dietary change could help in curing arthritis (Freeman, 1979), or the nutritionist who claims that the symptoms of arthritis, namely stiffness, pain, and reduced mobility of the joint, are cumulative reactions to allergic or toxic constituents in certain foods (Fredericks, 1981). Allergens that may produce arthritic episodes include: milk, pork, chocolate, wheat, eggs, beef, chicken, some fruits, and the food additive sodium nitrate. From my own experiences with skin and joint problems, I am convinced that any of the foods mentioned can cause arthropathies in some susceptible individuals. Unfortunately it is often nearly impossible to pinpoint the potential allergen or poison.

PHYSICAL THERAPY

Physical therapy, an essential part of therapy in any form of arthropathy, can play a major role in controlling pain, preventing deformity, and enhancing function (Bardwick, 1982). However, prolonged periods of professional therapy are not practical and the patient must eventually assume major responsibility for treating himself or herself at home. One should seek early medical advice and referral to a physical therapist in order to learn what treatment will help to maintain mobility, flexibility, and strength through passive and active exercises. The knowledge gained must then be used in applicable self-treatment. One should accept the fact, however, that physical therapy is not curative and will not ensure permanent relief (Schutt, 1977).

EXERCISE AND SPORTS

The philosophy that every human being needs regular physical activity to maintain optimal fitness and health also applies to the arthritic patient. However, the degree of the disease, the pain that can be tolerated temporarily, and the range of motion in the affected joint dictate the type and intensity of useful and desirable exercise. Depending on the seriousness of the disability, exercise needs to be modified:

1. In acute arthritis and also soon after joint surgery, exercise is to be passive; that is, someone else moves the limb in attempting to maintain or improve the range of motion;
2. Also in that stage, the strength of the muscles proximal and distal to the affected joint must be maintained or improved by isometric contractions that do not move the joint;
3. In chronic arthritis and degenerative osteoarthrosis, such isometric contractions are replaced by active resistive exercises, again to further improve the stabilizing or supportive strength of pertinent musculature;
4. And to the appropriate exercises are added general physical activities which are valuable for physical conditioning.

What exercise is either good or bad for a diseased joint? The resulting pain, or lack of it, dictates the answer. Even enjoyable exercise is not always free from temporary discomfort. But when pain will not abate within a reasonable time after ending the exercise, then either its type or its intensity and duration may cause more damage than benefit to the diseased joint.

Let's consider jogging as an example. Although jogging may not be the primary cause for the onset of degenerative changes in weight-bearing joints (Jorring, 1980; Puranen et al., 1975), it will certainly contribute to further damage to the articular cartilage tissue once its degradation has begun for whatever reason. Thus, physical activities and sports that require running, jumping, and fast movements with frequent quick stops and changing directions should be relinquished. In walking, the load on the weight-bearing joints should be reduced by using supporting canes, modified ski poles, or underarm crutches.

Neureuther (1981) has measured the amount of weight saving on the leg joints while walking with two ski poles, and found that it amounted to 10% on the horizontal plane and as much as 16% in uphill and downhill walking. In similar measurements, I came up with a load reduction of 10 kg during the weight transfer from one leg to the other, using ski poles alternatingly. If both poles are used simultaneously to support the weight transfer to one leg only, the load saving on the respective hip joint can be greatly increased. On a longer hike, the compressive stress on the weight-bearing joint would be diminished by several metric tons. Dr. Beckmann (1982), who directs the Terrain Spa in Ohlstadt, Germany, has all his patients walk with weight supporting devices, mostly ski poles. He advocates their use as a prophylactic measure for all people with joint pain in the lower extremities. I personally prefer the use of underarm crutches on longer hikes because the support to one or both legs can be more readily adjusted according to either pain or terrain condition.

The energy spent by individuals with osteoarthrosis of the hip has been measured during walking with and without weight-supporting devices, and was found to be nearly twice as high as for healthy controls (MacNicol, McHardy, & Chalmers, 1980; McBeath, Bahrke, & Balke, 1974). This means that an individual with such a joint handicap may require the last reserves of his or her cardiorespiratory and metabolic capacity to keep up with the leisurely pace of 3 mph set by a healthy friend. That becomes an important consideration when exercising with a patient who has a combined handicap of osteoarthrosis and heart disease. Fitness activities that are less jarring than running, and therefore better tolerated for many years, are skating and cross-country skiing. Even more ideal are bicycling, rowing, paddling and, of course, swimming.

TOTAL JOINT REPLACEMENT

Fortunately, a rather ideal solution has been developed during recent years for those who are suffering from crippling joint degeneration. When degeneration of the hips has progressed to the point of minimal mobility and persistent pain day and night, the surgical procedure of arthroplasty can restore a new life to a desperate patient. The new artificial joint, a metal ball rotating in a plastic acetabulum, is practically painless after the unavoidable damage done to bone and surrounding soft tissue has healed completely. Mobility returns to near normal. Although doctors usually advise going easy on the new joint, I have found that the same recommendations for continued physical activity apply as discussed in the previous paragraph.

CONCLUSION

Regular exercise remains essential for a person who suffers from any form of arthropathy. Specific exercises help maintain optimal mobility and adequate muscular strength in the afflicted parts of the body. Carefully chosen exercises stimulate the regeneration of cartilage and the production of synovial fluid required for joint lubrication. Also, physical activity helps prevent a loss of bone mass and an undesirable weight gain that might contribute to quicker joint degeneration. And a regular habit of appropriate physical activity is necessary to counteract functional debilitation that may result from prolonged rest. It might also be worthwhile to attempt nutritional changes to reduce allergic or poisonous reactions of the articular cartilage to certain foods.

REFERENCES

BARDWICK, P.A. Physical therapies in arthritis. *Arthritis Therapy*, 1982, **72**, 223-234.

BECKMANN, P. Auf Stoecke gestuetzt — vor Kruecken geschuetzt. [Weight support by ski poles prevents later need for crutches.] *Aerztliche Praxis*, 1982, **34**, 2977.

BERNHARD, G.C. Sick joints in well patients. *Journal of Occupational Medicine*, 1982, **24**, 277-282.

BLUESTONE, R. Sick joints in sick patients. *Journal of Occupational Medicine*, 1982, **24**, 277-282.

BULLOUGH, P.G. Pathologic changes associated with the common arthritides and their treatment. *Pathology Annual*, 1979, **14**(2), 69-105.

CRABBE, B., & Cilento, R. *Arthritis exercise book*. New York: Simon & Schuster, 1980.

DINGLE, J.T. Articular damage in arthritis and its control. *Annals of Internal Medicine*, 1978, **88**, 821-826.

FREDERICKS, C. *Arthritis—Don't learn to live with it*. New York: Grosset & Dunlap, 1981.

FREEMAN, J. *Arthritis: The new treatment*. Chicago: Contemporary Books, 1979.

GRANT-WHYTE, H. Joggitis, marathonitis and marathon mania. *South African Medical Journal*, 1980, **58**, 4; **59**, 849.

HANCOCK, D.A., Asiedu-Offei, S., Atkinson, P.J., Reed, G.W., & Wright, V. Femoral bone mass in patients with rheumatoid arthritis and osteoarthrosis. *Rheumatology and Rehabilitation*, 1978, **17**, 65-71.

JORRING, K. Osteoarthritis of the hip. *Acta Orthopaedica Scandinavica*, 1980, **51**, 523-530.

KLUNDER, K.B., Rud, B., & Hansen, J. Osteoarthritis of the hip and knee joint in retired football players. *Acta Orthopaedica Scandinavica*, 1980, **51**, 925-927.

KREWER, S., & Edgar, A. *The arthritis exercise book*. New York: Simon & Schuster, 1981.

LOWMAN, C.L. Posture. In *Encyclopedia of sport sciences and medicine*. New York: The MacMillan Company, 1971.

MacNICOL, M.F., McHardy, R., & Chalmers, J. Exercise testing before and after hip arthroplasty. *Journal of Bone and Joint Surgery*, 1980, **62B**, 326-330.

McBEATH, A.A., Bahrke, M., & Balke, B. Efficiency of assisted ambulation determined by oxygen consumption measurements. *Journal of Bone and Joint Surgery*, 1974, **56A**, 994-1000.

MILLER, C., & LeLieuvre, R.B. A method to reduce chronic pain in elderly nursing home residents. *The Gerontologist*, 1982, **22**, 314-317.

MURRAY, R.O., & Duncan, C. Athletic activity in adolescence as an etiological factor in degenerative hip disease. *Journal of Bone and Joint Surgery*, 1971, **53B**, 406-419.

NEFF, G. Physikalisch-physiotherapeutische Massnahmen zur Funktionellen Wiederherstellung bei Koxarthrose. [Physical physiotherapeutic treatment for functional reconditioning of coarthrosis.] *Muenchener Medizinische Wochenschrift*, 1978, **120**, 869-873.

NEUREUTHER, G. Der Skistock im Sommer. [The use of ski poles during summer.] *Muenchener Medizinische Wochenschrift*, 1981, **123**, 513-514.

NOAKES, T.D. Joggitis, marathonitis and marathon mania. *South African Medical Journal*, 1981, **60**, 84-86. (Response to Grant-Whyte.)

PURANEN, J., Ala-Ketola, L., Peltokallio, P., & Saarela, J. Running and primary osteoarthritis of the hip. *British Medical Journal*, May 1975, pp. 424-425.

SCHUTT, A.H. Physical medicine and rehabilitation in the elderly arthritis patient. *Journal of American Geriatrics Society*, 1977, **25**, 76-82.

VON DOMARUS, A. Grundriss der Inneren Medizin (9th ed.). Berlin: Julius Springer Verlag, 1935.

Exercise and Osteoporosis

Henry J. Montoye
University of Wisconsin—Madison

The term osteoporosis literally means more porous bones, and a number of medical problems result in varying degrees of osteoporosis. However, osteoporosis that results from these conditions is of limited interest to exercise scientists and health educators and is not considered in this review. Of much greater concern to us is the so-called "senile" or "post-menopausal" osteoporosis. These terms are inaccurate because, although it occurs to a greater extent in women, men are not immune. Furthermore, the onset in women frequently occurs before menopause and certainly before the age we associate with senility.

The loss in bone that occurs as we age is illustrated in Figure 1, drawn from data on residents of Ohio (Garn, 1970, p. 45). However, similar curves could be drawn for populations in Central America and Europe, populations which differ greatly in body size, activity level, diet, and disease prevalence (Garn, 1970, p. 49; Garn, Rohmann, & Wagner, 1967). Age changes in bone similar to those in the United States were even observed in a rural population in Ecuador known for their longevity (Mazess, 1978). Garn (1973) reviewed data on more than 20 populations around the world and found none that did not fail to lose bone in later adulthood. Although the data in Figure 1 represent the width of the cortical bone in the second metacarpal, a tubular bone, demineralization of bone is not confined to tubular or limb bones. Regardless of the population studied, females universally show much greater loss with age than males (Nordin, 1966). Apparently, as we age, cortical bone is laid down throughout life at the subperiosteal surface. After about age 30-40, it is lost from the endosteal surface at a faster rate than it is laid down in the outer surface of the bone.

Loss of hard (cortical) bone carries with it the increasing probability of bone fracture. Thus, the incidence of bone fractures increases with age in various populations (Chalmers & Ho, 1970), and this occurs

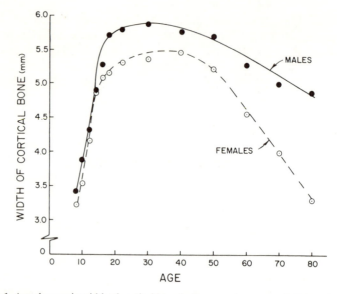

Figure 1. Age changes in width of cortical bone in the second metacarpal. Drawn from data of Garn (1970, p. 45).

despite the decrease in vigorous occupational and leisure activity by older people (Montoye, 1975, p. 20). The fractures in older women increase with age at a significantly higher rate than in males in many populations (Alffram, 1964; Alffram & Bauer, 1962; Bauer, 1960; Chalmers & Ho, 1970; Garn, 1973; Knowelden, Buhr, & Dunbar, 1964; Riggs, Wahner, Seeman, Offord, Dunn, Mazess, Johnson, & Melton, 1982). The problem goes beyond a fractured bone and confinement; about 20% of the women suffering a hip fracture die from complications, according to Drinkwater (1981). This supports the estimate of a mortality rate of 15 to 30% following fractures in postmenopausal women (Avioli, 1981).

TECHNIQUES OF STUDYING BONE

In animal studies and in human cadavers, it is possible to study the mechanical and chemical properties of bone directly. However, in live human beings, generally the only methods available are either the traditional x-ray or one of the newer scanning methods. One procedure for estimating cortical portion of a tubular bone such as the second metacarpal is explained in detail by Garn (1970). In this method, if some reasonable assumptions are made about the shape of the bone, the cross-sectional area of the cortical bone may be estimated from the diameter of the total bone and the diameter of the medullary cavity. Differences in density of the cortical bone are generally not discernible by this method.

Reproducibility of the length and width of the bone are excellent. However, reproducibility of the medullary diameter leaves something to be desired (Montoye, McCabe, Metzner, & Garn, 1976). Photodensitometry of radiographs has also been used, but with tissue-covered bones the error is 20-30%, which equals or exceeds the normal variation of the bone mineral content in many populations (Cameron, Mazess, & Sorenson, 1968).

The newer methods of scanning used one of several sources of energy. Probably the most useful is the device developed by Cameron and Sorenson (1963) which employs well-collimated radionuclide, iodine-125 (^{125}I) or americium-241 (^{241}Am). Called single-photon absorptiometry, the method is more precise and accurate than other techniques (Cameron et al., 1968). For example, ^{125}I scans on tissue-covered cadaver forearms correlated very highly with the dry weight ($r = 0.96$) and ash weight ($r = 0.96$) of the underlying bone. The method provides a very accurate measurement of the diameter as well as the mineral content of the bone.

PHYSICAL INACTIVITY AND BONE MINERAL

In a review by Booth and Gould (1975), much of the earlier work on the relationship of exercise to bone size and bone mineral was summarized. They reported that extreme inactivity in animals (casting, denervation, etc.) and in humans (paraplegics, bed rest, space flight, etc.) cause loss of bone. The remaining bone appears to be of normal composition; there is simply less of it and thus its strength is clearly decreased.

Since the review by Booth and Gould, other data on near weightlessness have been published, mainly from the joint USSR/USA Biosatellite mission on Kosmos 1129, flown September 24-October 14, 1979. Much of these data were published in supplements to volumes 23, 24, and 25 of *The Physiologist*. Data on rats reaffirmed that mineral is lost from weight-bearing bones (Cann, Adachi, & Morey-Holton, 1980; Heinrich & Souza, 1981; Kaplansky, Savina, Portugalov, Ilyina-Kakueva, Alexexev, Durnova, Pankova, Plakhuta-Plakutina, Shvets, & Yakovleva, 1980; Kotovskaya, Ilyin, Korolkov, & Shipov, 1980; Simmons, 1981; Turner, Bobyn, Duvall, Morey, Baylink, & Spector, 1981; Ushakov, Smirnova, Pitts, Pace, Smith, & Rahlmann, 1980; Wronski, Morey-Holton, & Jee, 1980). In space flight, bone loss in weight-bearing bones appears to be a matter of marked decrease in deposition on the subperiosteal surface with little change of resorption on the endosteal surface (Cann et al., 1980; Simmons, 1981; Turner et al., 1981; Wronski et al., 1980). In-flight centrifugation appears to eliminate the loss of mineral in weight-supporting bones (Kotovskaya et al., 1980; Spengler,

Morey, Carter, Turner, & Baylink, 1979). Unlike weight-bearing bones, the mandible of rats in space loses little, if any, mineral (Simmons, Russell, Winter, Baron, Vignery, Van Thuc, Rosenberg, & Walker, 1980). Van Huss and Heusner (1979) in their excellent review also point out that the calcium loss is much more severe in weight-supporting bones.

Doty and Morey-Holton (1982) found that in rats subjected to simulated weightlessness, there was reduced activity of the osteoblasts in the long bones. This suggests that the lack of mechanical stress somehow "signals" the osteoblasts not to function in their normal activity. Simulated weightlessness in rats also resulted in impaired transport of calcium from intestine to bone (Bikle, Globus, & Morey, 1982).

It is well known that immobilization of a limb after an injury results in bone loss. Typical was a report of 44 sports injuries involving the knee. In operated cases followed by casting, an 18% loss in bone mineral occurred; in unoperated cases the loss was 10%. After one year the bone mineral still had not returned to normal (Andersson & Nilsson, 1979). Because of this phenomenon, plates of varying bending stiffness were attached to the femurs of dogs to study the effects on osteopenia. Increasing stiffness of the plate caused increased loss of cortical bone and reduced bone strength (Bradley, McKenna, Dunn, Daniels, & Slatton, 1979; Woo, Kuei, Amiel, Gomez, Hayes, White, & Akeson, 1981). It appears that the bending loads to which the bone was subjected during healing shortened the healing time.

Studies in which one limb of an animal is immobilized and compared to the control limb have continued. From these studies it is clear that distal (and smaller) bones lose more mineral than the proximal bones and the loss is primarily at the periosteal surface (Uhthoff & Jaworski, 1978). When monkeys were restrained for 6 months, the usual bone loss occurred. Dietary calcium absorption decreased and calcium turnover increased, implying a rise in bone resorption compatible with the bone loss (Cann & Young, 1976).

EFFECT OF IMPOSED EXERCISE: ANIMAL STUDIES

All these are examples of total inactivity. But exercise relative to bone may function like some vitamins; a minimum is necessary but additional amounts may have no beneficial effect. On the other hand, exercise may have a direct and proportional effect—more than usual exercise may result in more cortical bone and greater breaking strength. Since the review by Booth and Gould (1975) there have been other animal studies.

Kiiskinen and Heikkinen (1975) found an increase in calcium content and breaking strength of the femur as a result of exercise in mice, but later Kiiskinen (1977) reported inconclusive results. Bell, Tzeng, and Draper (1980) reported increases in the total weight, ash weight, and cortical thickness of the tibia as a result of forced exercise in mice, but the differences from controls were not striking. Although one study (Kiiskinen & Heikkinen, 1975) showed a qualitative difference in the bones as a result of exercise, most studies continue to show only quantitative changes (Woo, Amiel, Akeson, Kuei, & Tipton, 1979; Woo et al. 1981). The intensity of exercise and age of the animals remains important in determining the effects of exercise on bone. Another confounding effect is the weight of the animals. The increase in weight (fat) can cause hypertrophy of bone (Pitts & Bullard, 1967), but even when paired in body fat exercise resulted in an increase in bone. The effects of body weight are illustrated in another study (Rosenfeld, Rosenfldová, Steiglová, & Kvapilová, 1973). Exercise in rats resulted in a decrease in absolute amount of calcium in the leg bones by 10-15%, but the body weights of the exercised animals were lower by 18%.

Beagles made to carry an extra load while walking on a treadmill developed significantly more mineral in the tibia (Martin, Albright, Clarke, & Niffenegger, 1981). Within 3 months following unilateral removal of the ulnar diaphsis in pigs, the cross-sectional area of the overstrained radius approached that of the ulna and the radius together in the contralateral limb (Goodship, 1979).

ATHLETES VS. NONATHLETES

Ryan, in the Academy papers of 1974, quoted an earlier study in which long-time soccer players were found to have femurs with greater diameters than controls. Similarly, Nilsson and Westlin (1971), using the photon-absorption method, found 64 young male athletes to have greater bone density in the distal end of the femur compared to 39 age-matched male nonathletes. Furthermore, among the athletes, the femur density was positively correlated with the load on the lower limbs demanded by the sport. Thus, the weight-lifters and throwers had the greatest density and swimmers did not differ from controls. Nonathletes who were more active had greater density than those who were sedentary. In a study by Dalén and Olsson (1974), 15 male cross-country runners (mean age, 55) had greater mineral content (g/cc.) at seven sites than 24 male controls (mean age of 53). Brewer, Meyer, Upton, and Hagen (1982) found the same results in females. Male weight lifters and male and female ballet dancers have greater mineral content in the tibia and fibula and the bones are wider than controls (Nilsson, Andersson, Havdrup, & Westlin, 1978). One group of athletes is of particular interest. Amenorrhea resulting from intensive athletic training may also cause bone loss (González, 1982) but more data are needed on this point before firm conclusions can be drawn.

Cross-sectional studies have also been done on people who vary in their habitual activity but who are not necessarily athletes. Montoye and others (1976) were not able to show significant difference in bone measurements among men aged 45-64, classified by habitual physical activity. However, a nonweight-supporting bone was studied and the x-ray method employed is less sensitive than photon absorptiometry. Using x-ray density measurement of the second phalangeal segment of the small finger, Emiola and O'Shea (1978) reported greater density in the more active people. However, grip strength was used in part to classify the subjects by habitual physical activity; hence body size could be responsible for the differences since grip strength is known to be related to body size. Borkan and Norris (1980) found no significant relationship between percent cortical bone and physical activity in nearly 1,000 males in the Baltimore Longitudinal Study. In 36 women with previous Colles' fractures, aged 50-73, bone mineral in the lumbar vertebrae was positively correlated with working capacity. The authors suggested that physical exercise might help prevent vertebral bone loss in these women (Krølner, Tøndevold, Toft, Berthelsen, & Nielsen, 1982).

Cross-sectional studies of the kind described in this section may be evidence that exercise causes an increase in bone mass. However, perhaps as plausible is the explanation that the mesomorphic, large-bone individual gravitates toward athletics and physical activity.

EXERCISE: LONGITUDINAL STUDIES IN HUMAN BEINGS

Usually in scientific studies of human beings, the longitudinal, experimental approach produces more definitive findings than in cross-sectional comparisons. This design is somewhat more difficult when studying bone changes because, although bone is a dynamic tissue, it still takes a long time before changes may be detected. Also, those old enough to suffer from "senile" osteoporosis may be more difficult to motivate to increase their habitual exercise. Nevertheless, some data have been reported. More than 30 years ago Freeman (1949) reported that the use of crutches reduced the excessive loss of calcium in paraplegics; however, therapeutic exercise and the use of wheelchairs did not. In poliomyelitis there is also extensive loss of bone but Plum and Dunning (1958) found that therapeutic exercise, short of walking, did not lessen hypercalciuria.

Dalén and Olsson (1974) followed 19 office workers (aged 25-52) for 3 months after beginning a walking or running program. Although their $\dot{V}O_2$max improved an average of 11%, there were no significant changes in bone at seven sites. But 3 months is a brief period to expect to see changes in bone. Aloia, Cohn, Ostuni, Cane, and Ellis (1978) observed no change in bone mineral of the distal radius in nine postmenopausal women after one year of exercise compared to controls. However, total body calcium increased in the exercise group and decreased in the control group, and the differences were statistically significant. Older women appear to have greater difficulty in absorbing and utilizing calcium because of decreased estrogen; hence, calcium supplementation perhaps should accompany exercise in an effort to increase bone mineral in this age group (Korcok, 1982).

Smith (1973) and Smith and Babcock (1973) reported the results of an 8-month study of 39 women, aged 55-94 years. The mineral content of the radius did not change in the controls, but the exercise group showed a statistically significant increase of 2.6%. Surprisingly, the physical therapy group showed an increase of 7.8%, which was significantly greater than in the exercise group. In later reports (Smith, 1982; Smith & Reddan, 1975; Smith, Reddan, & Smith, 1981), this group reported the results of a 36-month study of 30 women, mean age 84. Twelve exercise subjects engaged in mild activity 3 days per week and showed a 2.3% increase in bone mineral of the distal radius. Eighteen control subjects showed an average loss of 3.3%. The difference was statistically significant.

EXERCISE: STUDIES OF THE DOMINANT LIMB

There are several advantages in comparing the dominant to nondominant limb in studying the effects of exercise. Confounding factors such as inheritance and diet are controlled. Booth and Gould (1975) quoted an early observation (Kohlrausch, 1924) that bass viola players have abnormally large left hands compared to their right hands. They also mentioned the unusual case of a laborer whose thumb and all fingers of the right hand except the fifth finger had been amputated. Thirty-one years later the bones in this finger were wider and longer than the corresponding bones on the opposite hand (Ross, 1950). Buskirk, Andersen, and Brozek (1956) were among the first to make observations of the dominant vs. nondominant arms of tennis players. Roentgenograms were taken of both forearms of seven tennis players (mean age 24.7 years) and 11 soldiers (mean age 20.8 years). Widths of the radius and ulna were greater in the dominant arm in both groups, but the differences in the two arms were twice as great in the tennis players. The length of the ulna and radius of the dominant side was significantly greater in the tennis players by an average of 1.8%, but the difference averaged only 0.6% in the soldiers.

In a limited study of four professional players (Lewis, 1971), x-ray measurements showed "increase in osseous circumference and cortical width on the racquet-holding side. . . . There were no changes in the small bones of the hands and fingers." A much more extensive study of 84 young World Class professional tennis players was reported a few years later (Jones, Priest, Hayes, Technor, & Nagel, 1977; Priest, Jones, Technor, & Nagel, 1977). Using roentgenograms, the playing arm showed hypertrophy of the humerus. Depending on the site and sex of the player, the mean cortical thickness was increased from 25 to 29%. Measurements of the proximal radius and ulna showed similar differences between the dominant and nondominant arms but the average increase was less, 11%.

However, all of these studies are of young professional tennis players who practice many hours each day and have not reached an age where bone loss is a problem. An important question is whether recreational tennis playing, for example, an hour or two a day in an older population, would cause hypertrophy of the bones in the playing arm. In recent years the National *Senior* Clay Court Tennis Championships for men were held in Knoxville, Tennessee. The humerus, radius, and ulna of the playing arm was compared to the nonplaying arm using photon absorptiometry. Similarly, the second and third metacarpal bones in each hand were compared using traditional radiograms. The men averaged 64 years of age. They had been playing tennis for a mean of 40 years and average about 8 hours of tennis per week. The results are shown in Figure 2. Clearly there is an increase in width and mineral of the bones on the dominant side. Interestingly, the length of the metacarpals are also significantly greater on the dominant side (Montoye, Smith, Fardon, Howley, & Beauchene, 1979; Montoye, Smith, Fardon, & Howley, 1980). These results were later confirmed in 35 tennis players, age 70-84 years, in which the Cameron-Sorenson instrument was also used (Huddleston, Rockwell, Kulund, & Harrison, 1980).

The differences in the dominant vs. nondominant arms and hands are greater than those found in non-tennis players. For example, in the second metacarpal of the two hands of 131 males of the same age as the tennis players of Figure 2, the length was the same in both hands, the total cross-sectional area was greater in the dominant hand by only 2.8%, and the cortical cross-sectional area by 0.4% (Montoye et al., 1976). Similarly, Plato and Norris (1980) found differences of 5.5% and 0.6%, respectively.

Sosna (1970) compared the bones of the two limbs of 12 nationally ranked fencers. No significant differences in the dominant vs. nondominant side were found in the ulna, radius, or bones of the hand in this small sample. However, the report was sketchy so it is difficult to evaluate the methods. Nilsson and Westlin (1971) using the Cameron-

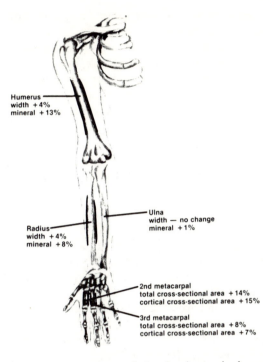

Humerus
width +4%
mineral +13%

Ulna
width — no change
mineral +1%

Radius
width +4%
mineral +8%

2nd metacarpal
total cross-sectional area +14%
cortical cross-sectional area +15%

3rd metacarpal
total cross-sectional area +8%
cortical cross-sectional area +7%

Figure 2. Comparison of bones in the two limbs of senior tennis players. Percentages indicate the increase in bone of the dominant (playing) arm and hand compared to the nondominant arm and hand (Montoye et al., 1980).

Sorenson method found no significant difference in bone mineral between femurs in the two legs of nonathletes. On the other hand, the mineral was significantly higher in the femur of the preferred leg among athletes. Watson (1973) compared the two upper limbs of 203 young male baseball players (age 8-19 years). Clearly the bones of the dominant arm were wider and contained more mineral, the differences in the humerus being greater and more consistent than in the ulna or radius. Finally, ballet dancers show hypertrophy of the second and third metatarsal as a result of the loads placed on these bones (Mostardi, Porterfield, & Greenberg, 1982).

RACIAL COMPARISONS

Blacks have fewer fractures of the femur per 1,000 individuals than do whites (Bauer, 1960; Bollet, Engh, & Parson, 1965; Gyepes, Mellias, & Katz, 1962; Smith & Rizek, 1966; Solomon, 1968) and osteoporosis is less of a problem in this race (Garn, 1973; Smith & Rizek, 1966). In a careful analysis of the skeletons of 40 white and 40 black cadavers, Trotter, Broman, and Peterson (1960) showed the bones of blacks to be denser than those of whites. Cohn, Abesamis, Yasumura, Aloia, Zanzi, and Ellis (1977) compared black and white females and reported that, despite no significant difference in stature in the two groups, black women had a greater skeletal and muscle mass and bone mineral content of the radius than age-matched whites. They concluded that the larger muscle mass in relation to height and weight in the blacks accounts for the difference.

MUSCLE STRENGTH AND BONE

Sinaki, Opitz, and Wahner (1974) measured the bone mineral of the radius in 161 normal men and women. They found no correlation between bone measurements and grip strength and tensiometer strength of the elbow flexors. We found no correlation between grip strength and second metacarpal bone measurements in 346 men, aged 45-64 years (Montoye et al., 1976). Plato and Norris (1980) using the same bone measurements reported weak correlations between grip strength and total width ($r = .20$ to .24) and cortical area ($r = .28$ to .34). As in our study, the effects of age and body size were removed. We also found no relationship between grip strength and bone measurements in senior tennis players (Montoye et al., 1980).

MECHANISM

All land animals evolved under the influence of the earth's gravity, which imposed adaptations that are apparent in animals of increasing size. Galileo in 1638 recognized that the load-bearing bones became greater in larger terrestrial animals in response to gravity but this did not occur in aquatic animals (Smith & Burton, 1980).

Almost a century ago Wolff (1892) suggested that mechanical stress applied to a bone causes architectural change, usually called remodeling. This has come to be known as Wolff's Law. Muscular exercise is thought to be a source of mechanical stress and thus results in bone changes. However, the mechanism has not been fully explained. The loss of bone in paralysis, for example, could be due to (a) decrease or absence of neural impulses (neurotrophic concept), (b) decrease in blood flow to the area since muscular exercise results in an increase in vascularity and metabolism in bones (Kiiskinen & Suominen, 1975), or (c) to a decrease in local generation of electrical potentials. Of course, a combination of two or all three mechanisms may act simultaneously.

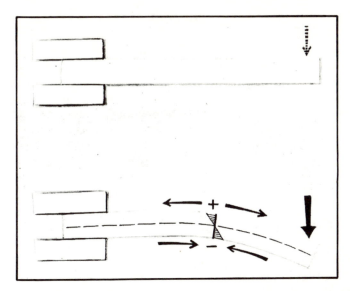

Figure 3. Illustration of electrical charges developing on bone surface as a result of deformation. Electronegativity develops on the concave surface; electropositivity on the convex surface. From Bassett (1971, p. 27).

The work of Bassett and Becker (1962) stimulated interest in the theory that local generation of electrical potential is responsible for bone changes with muscular exercise. They present evidence from other studies that mechanical factors have a direct action on osteogenic cells *in vitro*. They also point out that bioelectric or direct-current fields have been linked with cellular migration, tumor formation, and regeneration of amphibian limbs. Bone crystals are known to act like piezoelectric crystals and generate electrical potentials under pressure (Perren, 1968b). Bassett and Becker (1962) placed electrodes on opposite sides of freshly prepared long bones. When force was applied to bend the bone, the electrode on the concave side instantly became negative with respect to the electrode on the convex side of the bone. Equal bending of the bone in the opposite direction produced reversed polarity. This is illustrated in Figure 3. These results were produced in specimens of cat fibula, rat femur, and bullfrog tibiafibula. In a postscript to the paper, the authors acknowledge that, unknown to them, similar results had been observed several years earlier by Japanese investigators in 1957.

Various possibilities for explaining the mechanisms of how such electrical changes might affect bone were outlined by Perren (1968b) and Bassett (1971). The dynamic nature of bone has been further demonstrated by Perren (1968a) who, with very sensitive transducers, was able to show the existence of dimensional changes of tubular bones that are synchronized with heart beat and respiration.

SUMMARY

The development of a method of estimating bone mineral by direct photon absorptiometry by Cameron and Sorenson (1963) has made possible more definitive studies on exercise and bone in human beings. Highly trained athletes have larger bones (and hence more mineral) than controls not used to strenuous exercise. The bones in the dominant arm of professional tennis players are larger and contain more mineral than those in the nondominant arm. This is also true of senior amateur tennis players, but to a lesser degree. In both the professional and the amateur tennis players, the differences in bone between the two arms are greater than that found in non-tennis players of the same age.

Exercise among old people appears to delay some of the loss in bone mineral associated with aging. However, this conclusion must remain tentative until more intervention studies on older people are completed. Most recent studies of the effects of exercise in animals continue to show quantitative (i.e., an increase) rather than qualitative changes in bone. Thus, in animals and man, the size and mineral content of bones appears to be proportional to the exercise stimulus. Concerning the mechanism of bone changes brought about by muscular exercise, most investigators continue to subscribe to the hypothesis that muscular action results in mechanical stress on the bone. This, in turn, causes local generation of electrical potential which affects the balance of osteoblastic and osteoclastic activity.

REFERENCES

ALFFRAM, P. An epidemiologic study of cervical and trochanteric fractures of the femur in an urban population. *Acta Orthopaedica Scandinavica* (Suppl.), 1964, **65**, 1-109.

ALFFRAM, P., & Bauer, G.C.H. Epidemiology of fractures of the forearm. *Journal of Bone and Joint Surgery*, 1962, **44A**, 105-114.

ALOIA, J.F., Cohn, S.H., Ostuni, J.A., Cane, R., & Ellis, K. Prevention of involutional bone loss by exercise. *Annals of Internal Medicine*, 1978, **89**, 356-358.

ANDERSSON, S.M., & Nilsson, B.E. Changes in bone mineral content following ligamentous knee injuries. *Medicine and Science in Sports*, 1979, **11**, 351-353.

AVIOLI, L.V. Postmenopausal osteoporosis: Prevention versus cure. *Federation Proceedings*, 1981, **40**, 2418-2422.

BASSETT, C.A. Biophysical principles affecting bone structure. In G.H. Bourne (Ed.), *The biochemistry and physiology of bone*. New York: Academic Press, 1971.

BASSETT, C.A., & Becker, R.O. Generation of electric potentials by bone in response to mechanical stress. *Science*, 1962, **137**, 1063-1064.

BAUER, G. Epidemiology of fracture in aged persons. *Clinical Orthopaedics*, 1960, **17**, 219-225.

BELL, R.R., Tzeng, D.Y., & Draper, H.H. Long-term effects of calcium, phosphorus and forced exercise on the bones of mature mice. *Journal of Nutrition*, 1980, **110**, 1161-1167.

BIKLE, D.D., Globus, R.K., & Morey, E.R. Calcium transport from the intestine and into bone in a rat model simulating weightlessness. *The Physiologist* (Suppl.), 1982, **25**, 143-144.

BOLLET, A.J., Engh, G., & Parson, W. Epidemiology of osteoporosis. *Archives of Internal Medicine*, 1965, **116**, 191-194.

BOOTH, R.W., & Gould, E.W. Effects of training and disuse on connective tissue. In J.F. Keogh (Ed.), *Exercise and sports science reviews*. New York: Academic Press, 1975.

BORKAN, G.A., & Norris, A.H. Biological age in adulthood: Comparison of active and inactive males. *Human Biology*, 1980, **52**, 787-802.

BRADLEY, G.W., McKenna, G.B., Dunn, H.K., Daniels, A.V., & Slatton, W.O. Effects of flexural rigidity of plates on bone healing. *Journal of Bone and Joint Surgery*, 1979, **61A**, 866-872.

BREWER, V., Meyer, B., Upton, J., & Hagen, R.D. Role of exercise in prevention of involutional bone loss. *Medicine and Science in Sports and Exercise*, 1982, **14**, 106-107.

BUSKIRK, E.R., Andersen, K.L., & Brozek, J. Unilateral activity and bone and muscle development in the forearm. *Research Quarterly*, 1956, **27**, 127-131.

CAMERON, J.R., Mazess, R.B., & Sorenson, J.A. Precision and accuracy of bone mineral determination by direct photon absorptiometry. *Investigative Radiology*, 1968, **3**, 141-150.

CAMERON, J.R., & Sorenson, J. Measurement of bone mineral in vivo: An improved method. *Science*, 1963, **142**, 230-232.

CANN, C.E., Adachi, R.R., & Morey-Holton, E. Bone resorption and calcium absorption in rats during spaceflight. *The Physiologist* (Suppl.), 1980, **23**, S83-S86.

CANN, C., & Young, D.R. Bone formation rate in experimental disuse osteoporosis in monkeys (M. Nemestrina). *The Physiologist*, 1976, **19**, 147.

CHALMERS, J., & Ho, K.C. Geographical variations in senile osteoporosis. *Journal of Bone and Joint Surgery* (Br.), 1970, **52**, 667-675.

COHN, S.H., Abesamis, C., Yasumura, S., Aloia, J.F., Zanzi, I., & Ellis, K.J. Comparative skeletal mass and radial bone mineral content in black and white women. *Metabolism*, 1977, **26**, 171-178.

DALÉN, N., & Olsson, K.E. Bone mineral content and physical activity. *Acta Orthopaedica Scandinavica*, 1974, **45**, 170-174.

DOTY, S.B., & Morey-Holton, E.R. Changes in osteoblastic activity due to simulated weightlessness conditions. *The Physiologist* (Suppl.), 1982, **25**, 141-142.

DRINKWATER, B. Exercise and the post-menopausal woman. *Synopsis of the National Conference on Physical Fitness and Aging*, 1981, pp. 19-20.

EMIOLA, L., & O'Shea, J.P. Effects of physical activity and nutrition on bone density measured by radiographic techniques. *Nutrition Reports International*, 1978, **17**, 669-681.

FREEMAN, L.W. The metabolism of calcium in patients with spinal cord injuries. *Annals of Surgery*, 1949, **129**, 177-184.

GARN, S.M. *The earlier gain and later loss of cortical bone.* Springfield, IL: Charles C. Thomas, 1970.

GARN, S.M. Adult bone loss, fracture epidemiology and nutritional implications. *Nutrition*, 1973, **27**, 107-115.

GARN, S.M., Rohmann, C.G., & Wagner, B. Bone loss as a general phenomenon in man. *Federation Proceedings*, 1967, **26**, 1729-1736.

GONZALEZ, E.R. Premature bone loss found in some nonmenstruating sportswomen. *Journal of the American Medical Association*, 1982, **248**, 513-514.

GOODSHIP, A.E. Functional adaptation of bone to increased stress. *Journal of Bone and Joint Surgery*, 1979, **61A**, 539-546.

GYEPES, M., Mellias, H.Z., & Katz, I. The low incidence of fracture of the hip in the Negro. *Journal of the American Medical Association*, 1962, **181**, 1073-1074.

HEINRICH, M., & Souza, K. Summary of studies of weightlessness in the Cosmos 1129 satellite. *Federation Proceedings*, 1981, **40**, 608.

HUDDLESTON, A.L., Rockwell, D., Kulund, D.N., & Harrison, R.B. Bone mass in lifetime athletes. *Journal of the American Medical Association*, 1980, **244**, 1107-1109.

JONES, H.H., Priest, J.D., Hayes, W.C., Technor, C.C., & Nagel, D.A. Humeral hypertrophy in response to exercise. *Journal of Bone and Joint Surgery*, 1977, **59A**, 204-208.

KAPLANSKY, A.S., Savina, E.A., Portugalov, V.V., Ilyina-Kakueva, E.I., Alexexev, E.I., Durnova, G.N., Pankova, A.S., Plakhuta-Plakutina, G.I., Shvets, V.N., & Yakovleva, V.I. Results of morphological investigations aboard biosatellites Cosmos. *The Physiologist* (Suppl.), 1980, **23**, S51-S54.

KIISKINEN, A. Physical training and connective tissues in young mice—physical properties of Achilles tendons and long bones. *Growth*, 1977, **41**, 123-137.

KIISKINEN, A., & Heikkinen, E. Effect of prolonged physical training on the development of connective tissue in growing mice. In H. Howald & J.R. Poortmans (Eds.), *Metabolic adaptations to prolonged physical exercise*. Basel: Birkhauser, 1975.

KIISKINEN, A., & Suominen, H. Blood circulation of long bones in trained growing rats and mice. *European Journal of Applied Physiology*, 1975, **34**, 303-309.

KNOWELDEN, J., Buhr, A., & Dunbar, O. Incidence of fractures in persons over 35 years of age. *British Journal of Preventive and Social Medicine*, 1964, **18**, 130-141.

KOHLRAUSCH, W. Ueber Den Einfluss Funktioneller Beanspruchung Auf Das Langenwachstum von Knochen. [Concerning the influence of functional strain on the lengthening of bones.] *Muenchener Medizinische Wochenscrift*, 1924, **71**, 513-514.

KORCOK, M. Add exercise to calcium in osteoporosis prevention. *Journal of the American Medical Association*, 1982, **247**, 1106-1107.

KOTOVSKAYA, A.R., Ilyin, E.A., Korolkov, V.E., & Shipov, A.A. Artificial gravity in space flight. *The Physiologist* (Suppl.), 1980, **23**, S27-S29.

KRØLNER, B., Tøndevold, E., Toft, B., Berthelsen, B., & Nielsen, S.P. Bone mass of the axial and appendicular skeleton in women with Colles' fracture: Its relation to physical activity. *Clinical Physiology*, 1982, **2**, 147-157.

LEWIS, C.W.D. Who's for tennis? *New Zealand Medical Journal*, 1971, **74**, 21-24.

MARTIN, R.K., Albright, J.P., Clarke, W.R., & Niffenegger, J.A. Load-carrying effects on the adult beagle tibia. *Medicine and Science in Sports and Exercise*, 1981, **13**, 343-349.

MAZESS, R.B. Bone mineral in Vilcabamba, Ecuador. *American Journal of Roentgenology*, 1978, **130**, 671-674.

MONTOYE, H.L. *Physical activity and health: An epidemiologic study of an entire community.* Englewood Cliffs, NJ: Prentice-Hall, 1975.

MONTOYE, H.J., McCabe, J.F., Metzner, H.L., & Garn, S.M. Physical activity and bone density. *Human Biology*, 1976, **48**, 599-610.

MONTOYE, H.J., Smith, E.L., Fardon, D.F., & Howley, E.T. Bone mineral in senior tennis players. *Scandinavian Journal of Sports Sciences*, 1980, **2**, 26-32.

MONTOYE, H.J., Smith, E.L., Fardon, D.F., Howley, E.T., & Beauchene, R.E. Bone density in senior tennis players. *Federation Proceedings*, 1979, **39**, 945.

MOSTARDI, R., Porterfield, J.A., & Greenberg, B. The physiology of ballet dancing. *Federation Proceedings*, 1982, **41**, 1676.

NILSSON, B.E., Andersson, S.M., Havdrup, T., & Westlin, N.E. Ballet-dancing and weight-lifting—Effects on BMC. *American Journal of Roentgenology*, 1978, **131**, 541-542.

NILSSON, B.E., & Westlin, N.E. Bone density in athletes. *Clinical Orthopaedics and Related Research*, 1971, **77**, 179-182.

NORDIN, B.E.C. International patterns of osteoporosis. *Clinical Orthopaedics*, 1966, **45**, 17-30.

PERREN, S.M. The load washer and the bone. *Kistler Information Quarterly for Electrical Measurements and Mechanical Values*, No.2, February 1968. (a)

PERREN, S.M. The piezoelectric bone. *Kistler Information Quarterly for Electrical Measurements and Mechanical Values*, No.4, July 1968. (b)

PITTS, G.C., & Bullard, T.R. Effects of moderate exercise on body composition of the guinea pig. *Federation Proceedings*, 1967, **26**, 776.

PLATO, C.C., & Norris, A.H. Bone measurements of the second metacarpal and grip strength. *Human Biology*, 1980, **52**, 131-149.

PLUM, F., & Dunning, M.F. The effect of therapeutic mobilization of hypercalciuria following acute poliomyelitis. *Archives of Internal Medicine*, 1958, **101**, 528-536.

PRIEST, J.D., Jones, H.H., Technor, C.J.C., & Nagel, D.A. Arm and elbow changes in expert tennis players. *Minnesota Medicine*, 1977, **60**, 399-404.

RIGGS, B.L., Wahner, H.W., Seeman, E., Offord, K.P., Dunn, W.L., Mazess, R.B., Johnson, K.A., & Melton, L.J. III. Changes in bone mineral density of the proximal femur and spine with aging. *Journal of Clinical Investigation*, 1982, **70**, 716-723.

ROSENFELD, R., Rosenfldová, A., Steiglová, J., & Kvapilová, I. Effect of exercise or acceleration on calcium metabolism in rats. *Physiologia Bohemoslovaca*, 1973, **22**, 195-199.

ROSS, J.A. Hypertrophy of the little finger. *British Medical Journal*, 1950, **2**, 987.

RYAN, A.J. Supporting evidence from the field of medicine. *American Academy of Physical Education Papers*, 1974, **8**, 27-34.

SIMMONS, D.J. Adaptations of the rat skeleton of weightlessness and its physiological mechanisms. Results of animal experiments aboard the Cosmos-1129 biosatellite. *The Physiologist* (Suppl.), 1981, **24**, S65-S68.

SIMMONS, D.J., Russell, J.E., Winter, F., Baron, R., Vignery, A., VanThuc, T., Rosenberg, G.D., & Walker, W. Bone growth in the rat mandible during space flight. *The Physiologist* (Suppl.), 1980, **23**, S87-S90.

SINAKI, M., Opitz, J.L., & Wahner, H.W. Bone mineral content: Relationship to muscle strength in normal subjects. *Archives of Physical Medicine and Rehabilitation*, 1974, **55**, 508-514.

SMITH, A.H., & Burton, R.R. Gravitational adaptation of animals. *The Physiologist* (Suppl)., 1980, **23**, S113-S114.

SMITH, E.L. The effects of physical activity on bone in the aged. In R..B. Mazess (Ed.), *International Conference on Bone Mineral Measurement*. DHEW publication (NIH) #75-683, 1973, pp. 397-407.

SMITH, E.L. Exercise for prevention of osteoporosis: A review. *Physician and Sports Medicine*, 1982, **10**, 72-83.

SMITH, E.L., & Babcock, S.W. Effects of physical activity on bone loss in the aged. *Medicine and Science in Sports*, 1973, **5**, 68.

SMITH, E.L., & Reddan, W.G. The effects of physical activity on bone in the aged. *Medicine and Science in Sports*, 1975, **1**, 84.

SMITH, E.L., Reddan, W., & Smith, P.E. Physical activity and calcium modalities for bone mineral increase in aged women. *Medicine and Science in Sports and Exercise*, 1981, **13**, 60-64.

SMITH, R.W., & Rizek, J. Epidemiological studies of osteoporosis in women of Puerto Rico and southeastern Michigan with reference to age, race, national origin and other related or associated findings. *Clinical Orthopaedics*, 1966, **45**, 31-48.

SOLOMON, L. Osteoporosis and fracture of the femoral neck in the South African Bantu. *Journal of Bone and Joint Surgery*, 1968, **50B**, 2-13.

SOSNA, A. The influence of fencing on the limb musculature. In J. Kral (Ed.), *Physical fitness and its laboratory assessment*. Prague: Universitas Carolina Pragensis, 1970.

SPENGLER, D.M., Morey, E.R., Carter, D.R., Turner, R.T., & Baylink, D.J. Effect of spaceflight on bone strength. *The Physiologist*, 1979, **22**, 118.

TROTTER, M., Broman, G.E., & Peterson, R.R. Densities of bones of white and Negro skeletons. *Journal of Bone and Joint Surgery*, 1960, **42A**, 50-58.

TURNER, R.T., Bobyn, J.D., Duvall, P., Morey, E.R., Baylink, D.J., & Spector, M. Evidence for arrested bone formation during spaceflight. *The Physiologist* (Suppl.), 1981, **24**, S97-S98.

UHTHOFF, H.K., & Jaworski, Z.F. Bone loss in response to long-term immobilization. *Journal of Bone and Joint Surgery*, 1978, **60B**, 420-429.

USHAKOV, A.S., Smirnova, T.A., Pitts, G.C., Pace, N., Smith, A.H., & Rahlmann, D.F. Body composition of rats flown aboard Cosmos-1129. *The Physiologist* (Suppl.), 1980, **23**, S41-S44.

VAN HUSS, W.D., & Heusner, W.W. *Space flight research relevant to health, physical education, and recreation*. Washington, DC: U.S. Government Printing Office, NASA Catalog Number NAS 1, 1979, 19-148.

WATSON, R.C. Bone growth and physical activity in young males. In R. Mazess (Ed.), *International Conference on Bone Mineral Measurement*. DHEW Publication (NIH) #75-683, 1973, pp. 380-386.

WOLFF, J. *Das Gesetz Der Transformation Der Knochen*. [The law of bone transformation.] Berlin: A. Hirschwald, 1892.

WOO, S.L.-Y., Akeson, W.H., Coutts, R.D., Rutherford, L., Doty, D., Jemmott, G.F., & Amiel, E. A comparison of cortical bone atrophy secondary to fixation with plates with large differences in bending stiffness. *Journal of Bone and Joint Surgery*, 1976, **58A**, 190-195.

WOO, S.L.-Y., Amiel, D., Akeson, W.H., Kuei, S.C., & Tipton, C.W. Effect of long term exercise on ligaments, tendons and bones of swine. *Medicine and Science in Sports*, 1979, **11**, 105.

WOO, S.L.-Y., Kuei, S.C., Amiel, D., Gomez, M.A., Hayes, W.C., White, F.C., & Akeson, W.H. The effect of prolonged physical training on the properties of long bone: A study of Wolff's Law. *Journal of Bone and Joint Surgery*, 1981, **63A**, 780-787.

WRONSKI, T.S., Morey-Holton, E., & Jee, W.S.S. Cosmos 1129: Spaceflight and bone changes. *The Physiologist* (Suppl.), 1980, **23**, S79-S82.

Exercise and the Physiology of Aging

Herbert A. deVries
University of Southern California

PHYSIOLOGICAL CHARACTERISTICS
OF THE ELDERLY

Statistics on population trends for the United States indicate that we are rapidly becoming a nation of older people. The absolute number, as well as the proportion, of our older population is increasing rapidly. In evaluating the effects of the aging process on human performance, several problems arise. First, it is difficult to separate the effects of aging per se from those of concomitant disease processes (particularly cardiovascular problems) that become more numerous with age. Second, the sedentary nature of adult life in the United States makes it very difficult to find "old" populations to compare with "young" populations at equal activity levels. Third, very little work has been done on longitudinal studies of the same population over a period of time. Conclusions drawn from cross-sectional studies comparing various age groups must be accepted with reservations because the weaker biological specimens are not likely to be represented in as great numbers in the older populations tested as in the younger, due to a higher mortality rate.

Just as various individuals age at different rates, various physiological functions seem to have their own rates of decline with increasing age. Indeed, some functions do not seem to degenerate with age (Shock, 1961); under resting conditions, there seem to be no changes in blood sugar, blood pH, or total blood volume. In general, functions that involve the coordinated activity of more than one organ system decline most with age and, as might be expected, changes due to aging are most readily observed when the organism is stressed. Homeostatic readjustment is considerably slower with increasing age.

This paper is adapted from the paper "Guidelines for Physical Activity in the Elderly" presented to the National Conference on Physical Fitness and Sports for All sponsored by The President's Council on Physical Fitness and Sports, Washington, DC, 1981.

Age Changes in Muscle Function

Strength decreases very slowly during maturity. After the fifth decade strength decreases at a greater rate, but even at age 60 the loss does not usually exceed 10 to 20% of the maximum for men, with women's losses somewhat greater (Montoye & Lamphiear, 1977; Petrofsky & Lind, 1975). When maximal grip strength was investigated in 100 men who all did similar work in a machine shop, no change in either grip strength or endurance was found from age 22 to 62 (Petrofsky & Lind, 1975). These data suggest that in this age bracket, small losses with age may largely be due to disuse rather than a true aging effect. However, decrements in strength do occur in old age.

Changes at the Cellular Level. Animal studies have shown that important age changes occur at the cellular level. First is a loss of contractile elements, which accounts for the decrement in strength. That the loss could result from losses in motor nerve fibers has been ruled out in studies on rats, which have shown that while muscle fiber numbers may be about 25% less in old rats, no change occurs in nerve fibers (Gutman, Hanzlikova, & Jakoubek, 1968). The second important change at the cell level is a reduction in respiratory capacity, which accounts for losses in muscle endurance and capacity for recovery (Ermini, 1976). Recently it has also been shown that the loss in human muscle tissue with age can entirely account for the downward trend in basal metabolism, which has been an accepted fact in metabolic studies for nearly a century (Tzankoff & Norris, 1977).

Age and Capacity for Hypertrophy. In order to evaluate cellular hypertrophy, Goldspink and Howells (1974) taught hamsters to lift weights. After weight training for 5 weeks, the mean fiber area of the biceps in the young animals increased very significantly by 35.6%. The old animals increased by 17.7%, which was marginally significant. All signs of hypertrophy were lost in 15 weeks.

With respect to human strength gain, Moritani and deVries (1979) investigated the time course of strength gain through weight training in old and young men in order to define the contribution of hypertrophy and such neural factors as "disinhibition" to the total change in strength over a period of 8 weeks. Young and old men showed similar, significant percentage increases in strength, although the young made greater absolute gains. However, the physiological adaptations were quite different. While young subjects showed highly significant hypertrophy, the strength gained by the old men was almost entirely due to "learning" to achieve higher activation levels as measured by EMG methods.

Force-velocity and Other Aspects of Strength. Damon (1971) has shown that age decrements in strength exist whether measured in isometric, concentric, or eccentric muscle contraction, and also whether measured as maximal instantaneous force achieved or as a mean value over a finite time period. However, his work showed isotonic strength to be affected more than isometric. The maximum velocity produced against any given mass is less for the old than the young, although the shape of the force velocity curve is similar. Thus, loss of strength with age consists of two components: a decrease in ability to maintain maximum force statically, and a decrease in ability to accelerate mass.

Muscular Endurance. With respect to muscular endurance or fatigue rate, Evans (1971) has shown with the EMG fatigue curve technique that fatigue rate is significantly greater in the old than the young when holding isometric contractions of 20, 25, 30, 35, 40, or 45% of MVC.

Age and Cardiovascular Function

The effects of a lifetime of vigorous exercise upon the cardiovascular system have not yet been investigated extensively by scientific methods. However, evidence has been presented from observations on individuals who have trained very hard into old age. Clarence De Mar, the famous marathon runner, ran 12 miles every day and maintained this level of training throughout his lifetime. He was still competing in 25- and 26-mile marathons at age 65 and ran his last 15-kilometer race at 68, two years before his death (from cancer). The autopsy showed that this unusually strenuous exercise had not hurt his heart, but that the myocardium was unusually well developed, the valves were normal, and the coronary arteries were estimated to be two or three times normal size.

Maximum Heart Rate. The maximum heart rate attainable during exercise decreases with age. Maximum heart rate for young adults is usually between 190 and 200 beats per minute; in old age this value decreases gradually. The maximum heart rate in older adults can be estimated as follows: MAX HR = 220 − age. Data from animal studies suggest that the reduction in maximum heart rate with age is due to intrinsic changes in the myocardium itself rather than changes in neural influences (Corre, Cho, & Barnard, 1976).

Cardiac Output. The at-rest cardiac output declines approximately 1% per year after maturity (Brandfonbrener, Landowne, & Shock, 1955). This evidence is supported by the fact that the strength of the myocardium measured by ballistocardiography declines at a similar rate (Starr, 1964). The most important parameter is the capacity for cardiac output at maximal exercise, which appears to decrease at a rate similar to resting cardiac output (Julius, Amery, Whitlock, & Conway, 1967).

Changes in Pulmonary Function

Lung Volumes and Capacities. It has been firmly established that vital capacity declines with age (Norris, Shock, Landowne, & Falzone, 1956;

Norris, Shock, & Falzone, 1962; Robinson, 1938). There appears to be no good evidence for any change in total lung capacity and, consequently, residual volume increases with age (Norris et al., 1956; Norris et al., 1962). Aging increases the ratio of RV/TLC, and anatomic dead space also increases with age (Comroe, Forster, Dubois, Briscoe, & Carlsen, 1962).

Thoracic Wall Compliance. Some tissues of the lungs and chest wall have the property of elasticity. Thus in inspiration the muscles must work against this elasticity, which then aids the expiration phase through elastic recoil. The relationship between force required (elastic force) per unit stretch of the thorax is called "compliance." It is measured by the size of the ratio of volume change per unit of pressure change. It may be thought of as the elastic resistance to breathing. That is to say, the less compliant the tissues, the more elastic force must be overcome in breathing. Two tissues offer elastic resistance to breathing: the lung tissue itself and the wall of the thoracic cage. Evidence suggests that lung compliance increases with age (Turner, Mead, & Wohl, 1968), but, more important, thoracic wall compliance decreases (Mittman, Edelman, Norris, & Shock, 1965; Rizzato & Marazzini, 1970; Turner et al., 1968). Thus the older individual may do as much as 20% more elastic work at a given level of ventilation than the young, and most of the additional work would involve moving the chest wall (Turner et al., 1968). It seems likely that the differences in lung volumes and capacities can be explained largely on the basis of this lessening mobility of the chest wall with age.

Pulmonary Diffusion. There is a significant decrease in the capacity for pulmonary diffusion, both at rest and at any given work load, which accompanies the aging process (Donevan, Palmer, Varvis, & Bates, 1959).

Ventilatory Mechanics in Exercise. In view of the changes in pulmonary function already cited, it is not surprising to find that the process of breathing becomes less efficient with age. Work from our laboratory shows clearly the need for greater ventilation in older men compared with young men at any given level of work or oxygen consumption (deVries, 1972). Interestingly, old subjects used different mechanics to meet the increased ventilatory demand. While the young first increased breathing frequency, the older men increased their tidal volume (the more efficient mechanism), thus reaching their maximal TV early at work loads where the young still had large reserves of TV for work at higher loads.

Age and Physical Working Capacity

Maximal Oxygen Consumption. The best single measure of physical working capacity (PWC) is "maximal oxygen consumption," and two excellent studies have related this variable to age. Robinson (1938) tested 79 males from 6 to 75 years of age and Astrand (1960) tested 44 women from 20 to 65 years of age; these results show similar age changes.

For adults of both sexes, maximal oxygen consumption declines gradually with age. For men, the maximal values were found at mean age 17.4 years and they declined to less than half those values at mean age 75. For women, the maximal values were found in the age group 20 to 29 and they fell off by 29% in the age group 50 to 65.

More recent data suggest that for both men (Dehn & Bruce, 1972) and women (Drinkwater, Horvath, & Wells, 1975), the rate of decline may be slower in those who are physically active. Kasch and Wallace (1976) have provided longitudinal data suggesting that the usual 9-15% decline in VO_{2max} from age 45 to 55 can be forestalled by regular endurance exercise. Hodgson and Buskirk (1977) have summarized the data from many cross-sectional studies, which suggest that active athletic subjects start at higher values and at age 60 are still at or above the level of the sedentary 20-year-olds, although the rate of decline is similar.

It is interesting to consider the physiological functions whose decline, with increasing age, might contribute to the loss of ability to transport and utilize oxygen. The following functions are probably the most important in achieving maximal oxygen consumption: a) lung ventilation; b) lung diffusion capacity for oxygen; c) heart rate; d) stroke volume; and e) oxygen utilization by the tissues. Direct and indirect evidence suggests that all these functions decline with age.

Age and the Nervous System

Age changes that slow reaction time and speed of movement have been verified. Birren and his co-workers (Birren, Butler, Greenhouse, Sokoloff, & Yarrow, 1963; Birren, Imus, & Winde, 1959), who have done extensive investigation in this area, have concluded that psychomotor slowing is probably due to the aging of the central nervous system because the slowing is common to several sensory modalities and to several motor pathways. The decreases in conduction time, both afferent and efferent, are insufficient to account for total slowing. Recent work suggests that a lifestyle of vigorous physical activity has a beneficial effect in lessening the decline in reaction and movement times (Clarkson, 1978; Spirduso, 1975).

Brain tissue is much more vulnerable to circulatory deficits than most tissues; it must have a constant source of oxygen and it cannot function anaerobically (as can muscle tissue, for instance). For this reason one is tempted to associate the effects of aging with a decreased cerebral blood flow and the resulting hypoxia. However, when the effects of aging per se are separated from the effects of arteriosclerosis that frequently accompanies the aging process, it appears the arteriosclerosis is at fault. Aging per se in the absence of arteriosclerotic changes probably does not result in circulatory or metabolic changes in cerebral function (Birren et al., 1959; Birren et al., 1963).

The German neurophysiologists, C. and O. Vogt (1946), have observed that the degree of activity of a particular type of nerve cell has a great effect on its aging process. They have found that involution (part of the aging process) "is delayed not only by normal but also by such excessive activity of nerve cells as results in their hypertrophy" (p. 304). This suggests that physical activity involving overuse of neural pathways of the central nervous system may have beneficial effects ·such as we know occur with muscle tissue. The Vogts' work has received support from Retzlaff and Fontaine (1965), who found improved spinal motor neuron function as the result of conditioning in rats. Much more scientific research on the possible benefits of vigorous exercise for aging populations is needed.

Age and Body Composition

It is typical for aging humans to gain weight, and Brozek (1952) has provided interesting data on the composition of the human body as it ages. In Brozek's sample it is clear that this weight gain represents a mean increase of 12.24 kilograms (27 pounds) of fat while the fat-free body weight has actually decreased from age 20 to 55. It is obvious that to maintain a constant proportion of body fat as one ages, weight must not merely be maintained, but decreased. It is conceivable, however, that the loss in fat-free weight represents disuse atrophy of muscle tissue and may not be a necessary component of aging changes if vigorous exercise is maintained.

Shock and his co-workers (Shock, Watkin, Yiengst, Norris, Gaffney, Gregerman, & Falzone, 1963) have furnished compelling evidence that this loss of active tissue is what causes the well-known decline in the basal metabolic rate (BMR) with age. When they computed BMR on the basis of body water (which reflects the amount of active tissue cells in the body), no significant changes were observed in relation to age. The customary method of calculating BMR (per unit of surface area) does not differentiate between fat and active tissue; thus we find that the aging body contains fewer and fewer cells, although the activity of individual cells probably does not change significantly. Again, we would like to know the effects vigorous exercise programs might have on this process.

Stature. It has been shown that, on the average, we also become shorter as we grow older and fatter. De Queker, Baeyens, and Claessens (1969) showed the loss rate to average about one-half inch per decade after age 30.

BENEFITS OF EXERCISE

It must be emphasized that all of the changes described thus far can be said only to *accompany* the aging process. Causal relationships have not been established. Observations of different groups of subjects at increasing age levels indicate that changes in the various functional capacities may result from a combination of at least three factors: true aging phenomena, unrecognized disease processes whose incidence and severity increase with age, and our increasingly sedentary lifestyle as we grow older. Since we can do little to modify the first two factors, and since the third factor can be modified by the methods of conditioning and training already well known to our profession, other investigators and I have addressed the question of "how trainable is the older human organism?"

Only recently have we turned to the problem of maintaining and improving physical fitness and associated functional capacities in the elderly male and female, arbitrarily defined here as the age bracket over 60. Table 1 shows the results of recent research in this direction.

There seems little doubt that the physical working capacity of the older individual can be improved by very significant increments. While this improved PWC may not add years to our life, it most certainly does add life to our years. The improvement of PWC is tantamount to increasing the vigor of the older individual, which can make an important contribution to the later years, certainly in terms of lifestyle and possibly even health.

Important effects of physical conditioning on bone and connective tissues have also been reported. A very serious problem for older people,

Table 1

Effects of Physical Conditioning on the Functional Capacities of Older Men and Women (Mean Age over 60)

Measurement	Sex	N	% improvement	Source*
Cardiovascular system				
1. Decrease in HR	M	5	19	Barry et al. (1966)
at submaximal	F	3		
work	M	8	3-5	Niinimaa & Shephard (1978)
	F	7	3	Niinimaa & Shephard (1978)
2. O_2 pulse	M	13	11	Benestad (1965)
	M	48	4 (6 weeks)	deVries (1971)
	M	5	29 (42 weeks)	deVries (1971)
	F	17	7 (12 weeks)	Adams & deVries (1973)
	M	8	1-5 (11 weeks)	Niinimaa & Shephard (1978)
	F	7	0-3 (11 weeks)	Niinimaa & Shephard (1978)

3. Increased blood volume	M	13	9	Benestad (1965)
4. Increased total Hb	M	13	7	Benestad (1965)
5. Cardiac output at submaximal work	M	34	0	deVries (1971)
	M	8	9	Niinimaa & Shephard (1978)
	F	7	0	Niinimaa & Shephard (1978)
6. Stroke volume at submaximal work	M	34	6	deVries (1971)
	M	8	0	Niinimaa & Shephard (1978)
	F	7	0	Niinimaa & Shephard (1978)
7. Resting systolic BP	M	5	13	Barry et al. (1966)
	F	3	13	
	M	66	2	deVries (1971)
	F	17	0	Adams & deVries (1973)
8. Resting diastolic BP	M	5	6	Barry et al. (1966)
	F	3	6	
	M	66	4	deVries (1971)
	F	17	0	Adams & deVries (1973)
9. Regression of ECG abnormalities	M	5	50% of abnormalities definitely improved	Barry et al. (1966)
	F	3		

Respiratory system

1. Vital capacity	M	5	0	Barry et al. (1966)
	F	3		
	M	66	5 (6 weeks)	deVries (1971)
	M	8	20 (42 weeks)	deVries (1971)
	F	17	0	Adams & deVries (1973)
2. Maximum ventilation during exercise	M	47	12 (6 weeks)	deVries (1971)
	M	7	35 (42 weeks)	deVries (1971)
	M	5	50	Barry et al. (1966)
	F	3	50	
	M	13	0	Benestad (1965)
	F	17	0	Adams & deVries (1973)
Physical work capacity, VO_{2max}	M	61	9 (6 weeks)	deVries (1971)
	M	8	16 (42 weeks)	deVries (1971)
	F	17	37	Adams & deVries (1973)
	M	5	76	Barry et al. (1966)
	F	3	76	
	M	14	29	Sidney & Shephard (1978)
	F	28	29	Sidney & Shephard (1978)
	M	14	11	Suominen et al. (1977)
	F	12	12	Suominen et al. (1977)
Muscular strength	M	68	6 (6 weeks)	deVries (1971)
	M	8	12 (42 weeks)	deVries (1971)
	M	5	50	Perkins & Kaiser (1962)
	F	15	50	

*Complete source data are given in the references section at the end of the chapter.

especially older women, is the loss of bony tissue (osteoporosis). Smith and Reddan (1977) showed that 20 women with a mean age of 82 gained 4.2% in bone mineral composition as the result of exercise compared with controls who lost 2.5% over the 36-month experimental period. Losses of joint mobility constitute another serious problem for the elderly. Again, appropriate exercise can result in significant improvement (Chapman, deVries, & Swezey, 1972).

The tranquilizer effect of exercise was compared with that of meprobamate (Miltown or Equanil) in our laboratory with respect to reduction of muscle action potential (MAP) level in 10 elderly "anxious" subjects (deVries & Adams, 1972). Thirty-six observations were made of each subject before and after (immediately, 30 minutes, and 1 hour after) each of five treatment conditions: a) meprobamate, 400 mg; b) placebo, 400 mg. lactose; c) 15 minutes "walking type" exercise at HR of 100 (moderate walking for elderly); d) 15 minutes of exercise at HR of 120; and e) resting control. Conditions 1 and 2 were administered double blind.

Exercise at HR of 100 lowered the electrical activity in the musculature by 20%, 23%, and 20% at the first, second, and third posttests, respectively. These changes significantly differed from controls at $P < 0.01$. Neither meprobamate nor placebo treatments were significantly different from controls. Exercise at the higher HR was only slightly less effective, but the data were more variable and approached but did not achieve significance.

Our data suggest that the tranquilizer effect may be one of the more important exercise benefits for anxious elderly subjects because exercise can avoid the further impairment of motor coordination, reaction time, and driving performance which may already be compromised in this age group. A 15-minute walk at a moderate rate appears to be sufficient stimulus to bring about the desired effect which persists for at least 1 hour afterward.

FITNESS CONSIDERATIONS
OTHER THAN AEROBIC CAPACITY

In many, if not in most, senior centers where group fitness programs are considered, physiological and/or medical monitoring are unavailable. This of course reduces the options for program content but does not eliminate the desirability of programs of lower levels of metabolic demand. Such activities as Yoga, stretching calisthenics, relaxation exercises, mild walking, and dancing will at least contribute to the joy of life and may well contribute to physiological improvement also. It is reasonable to believe the important benefits to joint mobility, muscle strength and endurance, and ability to relax may ensue from even the very mild calisthenic programs that are becoming more popular, but there is little research data supporting this position. The aerobic benefits from moderate walking and dancing are most firmly established for the middle-aged and young elderly, but little scientific evidence is available with respect to those over 60.

In the interests of safety and the prevention of medico-legal liability, even the participants in mild exercise programs should be taught the heart-rate monitoring procedures. In our experience (using radio telemetry methods), normal ambulatory older men and women will elicit heart rates of 100-120 in such everyday activities as walking and stair climbing. Therefore, an exercise leader would not be guilty of imprudent behavior if healthy, normal, asymptomatic older men and women worked to that level in a mild exercise program. However, this assumption has not been put to the test of litigation so far as I know.

SAFETY CONSIDERATIONS FOR SPORTS ACTIVITY

Depending upon the health of the individual, an increase or decrease in both intensity and duration of work load is indicated. Most activities allow for adjustments without complete cessation. In tennis and badminton, one plays doubles instead of singles; in skiing, one skis for shorter periods of time with longer intervals for rest, and so forth. Obviously, in all competitive dual sports, one modification is simply to play opponents of roughly equivalent age.

There is no evidence that vigorous exercise can injure a healthy, older individual. However, frequent physical examinations, at least yearly, are necessary to protect the individual from overstrain during an incipient illness.

Indeed, a growing body of experimental evidence shows that the healthy older individual improves his or her functional capacities through physical conditioning much as the young person does. The improvement is comparable to that in the young, although the older person starts at and progresses to lower achievement levels and probably requires less training stimulus to bring about the desired response. In general, the effects of physical conditioning upon the middle-aged and older individual counter the effects commonly associated with the aging process.

REFERENCES

ADAMS, G.M., & deVries, H.A. Physiological effects of an exercise training regimen upon women aged 52-79. *Journal of Gerontology*, 1973, **28**, 50-55.

ASTRAND, I. Aerobic work capacity in men and women with special reference to age. *Acta Physiologica Scandinavica*, 1960, **49**, 169.

BARRY, A.J., Daly, J.W., Pruett, E.D.R., Steinmetz, J.R., Page, H.F., Birkhead, N.C., & Rodahl, K. The effects of physical conditioning on older individuals. *Journal of Gerontology*, 1966, **21**, 182-191.

BENESTAD, A.M. Trainability of old men. *Acta Medica Scandinavica*, 1965, **178**, 321-327.

BIRREN, J.E., Butler, R.N., Greenhouse, S.W., Sokoloff, L., & Yarrow, M.R. (Eds.), *Human aging, a biological behavioral study*. Washington, DC: Public Health Service Publication No. 986, 1963.

BIRREN, J.E., Imus, H.A., & Winde, W.F. (Eds.), *The process of aging in the nervous system*, Springfield, IL: C.C. Thomas, 1959.

BRANDFONBRENER, M., Landowne, M., & Shock, N.W. Changes in cardiac output with age. *Circulation*, 1955, **12**, 566-577.

BROZEK, J. Changes of body composition in man during maturity and their nutritional implications. *Federation Proceedings*, 1952, **11**, 784-793.

CHAPMAN, E.A., deVries, H.A., & Swezey, R. Joint stiffness: Effects of exercise on old and young men. *Journal of Gerontology*, 1972, **27**, 218-221.

CLARKSON, P.M. The effect of age and activity level on fractionated response time. *Medicine and Science in Sports*, 1978, **10**, 66.

COMROE, J.H., Forster, R.E., Dubois, A.B., Briscoe, W.A., & Carlsen, E. *The lung*. Chicago: The Yearbook Publishers, 1962.

CORRE, K.A., Cho, H., & Barnard, R.J. Maximum exercise heart rate reduction with maturation in the rat. *Journal of Applied Physiology*, 1976, **40**, 741-744.

DAMON, E.L. *An experimental investigation of the relationship of age to various parameters of muscle strength*. Unpublished doctoral dissertation, University of Southern California, 1971.

DEHN, M.M., & Bruce, R.A. Longitudinal variations in maximum oxygen intake with age and activity. *Journal of Applied Physiology*, 1972, **33**, 805-807.

DE QUEKER, J.V., Baeyens, J.P., & Claessens, J. The significance of stature as a clinical measurement of aging. *Journal of the American Geriatrics Society*, 1969, **17**, 169-179.

deVRIES, H.A. Physiological effects of an exercise training regimen upon men aged 52-88. *Journal of Gerontology*, 1970, **25**, 325-336.

deVRIES, H.A. Exercise intensity threshold for improvement of cardiovascular-respiratory function in older men. *Geriatrics*, 1971, **26**, 94-101.

deVRIES, H.A. Prescription of exercise for older men from telemetered exercise heart rate data. *Geriatrics*, 1971, **26**, 102-111.

deVRIES, H.A. Comparison of exercise responses in old and young men: II. Ventilatory mechanics. *Journal of Gerontology*, 1972, **27**, 349-352.

deVRIES, H.A., & Adams, G.M. Electromyographic comparison of single doses of exercise and meprobamate as to effects on muscular relaxation. *American Journal of Physical Medicine*, 1972, **51**, 130-141.

deVRIES, H.A., & Adams, G.M. Effect of the type of exercise upon the work of the heart in older men. *Journal of Sports Medicine and Physical Fitness*, 1977, **17**, 41-47.

DONEVAN, R.E., Palmer, W.H., Varvis, C.J., & Bates, D.V. Influence of age on pulmonary diffusing capacity. *Journal of Applied Physiology*, 1959, **14**, 483-492.

DRINKWATER, B.L., Horvath, S.M., & Wells, C.L. Aerobic power of females, age 10-68. *Journal of Gerontology*, 1975, **30**, 385-394.

ERMINI, M. Aging changes in mammalian skeletal muscle. *Gerontology* (Basel), 1976, **22**, 301-316.

EVANS, S.J. *An electromyographic analysis of skeletal neuromuscular fatigue with special reference to age*. Unpublished doctoral dissertation, University of Southern California, 1971.

GOLDSPINK, G., & Howells, K.F. Work induced hypertrophy in exercised normal muscles of different ages and the reversibility of hypertrophy after cessation of exercise. *Journal of Physiology*, 1974, **239**, 179-193.

GUTMAN, E., Hanzlikova, V., & Jakoubek, B. Changes in the neuromuscular system during old age. *Experimental Gerontology*, 1968, **3**, 141-146.

HODGSON, J.L., & Buskirk, E.R. Physical fitness and age: With emphasis on cardiovascular function in the elderly. *Journal of the American Geriatrics Society*, 1977, **25**, 385-392.

JULIUS, S., Amery, A., Whitlock, L.S., & Conway, J. Influence of age on the hemodynamic response to exercise. *Circulation*, 1967, **36**, 222-230.

KASCH, F.W., & Wallace, J.P. Physiological variables during 10 years of endurance exercise. *Medicine and Science in Sports*, 1976, **8**, 5-8.

MITTMAN, C., Edelman, N.H., Norris, A.H., & Shock, N.W. Relationship between chest wall and pulmonary compliance and age. *Journal of Applied Physiology*, 1965, **20**, 1211-1216.

MONTOYE, H.J., & Lamphiear, D.E. Grip and arm strength in males and females, age 10-69. *Research Quarterly*, 1977, **48**, 109-120.

MORITANI, T., & deVries, H.A. Potential for gross muscle hypertrophy in older men. *Journal of Gerontology*, 1980, **35**, 672-682.

NIINIMAA, V., & Shephard, R.J. *Journal of Gerontology*, 1978, **33**, 362-367.

NORRIS, A.H., Shock, N.W., & Falzone, J.A. Relation of lung volumes and maximal breathing capacity to age and socio-economic status. In H.T. Blumenthal (Ed.), *Medical and clinical aspects of aging*. New York: Columbia University Press, 1962.

NORRIS, A.H., Shock, N.W., Landowne, M., & Falzone, J.A. Pulmonary function studies: Age differences in lung volume and bellows function. *Journal of Gerontology*, 1956, **11**, 379-387.

PERKINS, L.C., & Kaiser, H.L. Results of short term isotonic and isometric exercise programs in persons over sixty. *Physical Therapy Review*, 1962, **41**, 633-635.

PETROFSKY, J.S., & Lind, A.R. Aging, isometric strength and endurance, and cardiovascular responses to static effort. *Journal of Applied Physiology*, 1975, **38**, 91-95.

RETZLAFF, E., & Fontaine, J. Functional and structural changes in motor neurons with age. In A.T. Welford & J.E. Birren (Eds.), *Behavior aging and the nervous system*. Springfield, IL: C.C. Thomas, 1965.

RIZZATO, G., & Marazzini, L. Thoracoabdominal mechanics in elderly men. *Journal of Applied Physiology*, 1970, **28**, 457-460.

ROBINSON, S. Experimental studies of physical fitness in relation to age. *Arbeitsphysiologie*, 1938, **10**, 251-323.

SHOCK, N.W. Current concepts of the aging process. *Journal of the American Medical Association*, 1961, **175**, 654-656.

SHOCK, N.W., Watkin, D.M., Yiengst, M.J., Norris, A.H., Gaffney, G.W., Gregerman, R.I., & Falzone, J.A. Age differences in the water content of the body as related to basal oxygen consumption in males. *Journal of Gerontology*, 1963, **18**, 1-8.

SIDNEY, K.H., & Shephard, R.J. Frequency and intensity of exercise training for elderly subjects. *Medicine and Science in Sports*, 1978, **10**, 125-131.

SMITH, E.L., & Reddan, W. Physical activity — A modality for bone accretion in the aged. *American Journal of Roentgenology Radium Therapy and Nuclear Medicine*, 1977, **126**, 1297.

SPIRDUSO, W.W. Reaction and movement time as a function of age and physical activity level. *Journal of Gerontology*, 1975, **30**, 435-440.

STARR, I. An essay on the strength of the heart and on the effect of aging upon it. *American Journal of Cardiology*, 1964, **14**, 771-783.

SUOMINEN, H., Heikinen, E., Liesen, H., Michel, D., & Hollmann, W. *European Journal of Applied Physiology*, 1977, **33**, 173-180.

TURNER, J.M., Mead, J., & Wohl, M.E. Elasticity of human lungs in relation to age. *Journal of Applied Physiology*, 1968, **25**, 664-671.

TZANKOFF, S.P., & Norris, A.H. Effect of muscle mass decrease on age-related BMR changes. *Journal of Applied Physiology*, 1977, **43**, 1001-1006.

VOGT, C., & Vogt, O. Aging of nerve cells. *Nature*, 1946, **158**, 304.

Exercise as a Factor in Aging Motor Behavior Plasticity

Waneen Wyrick Spirduso
The University of Texas

Human beings display incredible individual differences in many motor behaviors as they age. Some factors such as personality traits and verbal comprehension, if studied from a within-subjects perspective, seem resistant to age effects. Vocabulary may even improve over time (Katzman & Terry, 1982). Yet psychomotor speed is undeniably slower in older individuals.

Performance is slower in aged individuals on psychomotor tasks such as the Digit Symbol task (Weschler, 1958), tapping in place (Katzman & Terry, 1982), tapping two targets alternately (Welford, 1977), and moving a lever from side to side (Birren, Woods, & Williams, 1979). Even simple motor tasks such as crossing off symbols, copying, and tracing are slower (Birren et al., 1979; Storandt, 1976; Welford, 1977). Writing speed also slows.

Particularly dramatic is the decline in response speed that occurs in simple and choice reaction time (Birren et al., 1979) and in performance on tasks that require the coordination of two movements simultaneously (Rabbitt & Rogers, 1965). In fact, the more complex the choice reaction time task, the greater the reactivity deficits that are seen in the elderly (Cerella, Poon, & Williams, 1980). Choice reaction time paradigms that require spatial or symbolic transformations produce slower reaction times than those requiring no transformations, and faster reaction times than those involving both spatial and symbolic transformations.

The question is not whether psychomotor performance declines with age, but what motor control mechanisms are responsible for the decline. Weiss (1965) addressed the issue of motor versus perceptual-cognitive deterioration directly by recording premotor and motor components electromyographically. He reported that both premotor latency and motor time change, but that the perceptual-cognitive component (premotor latency) changes relatively more and accounts for most of the changes seen in tests of behavioral response speed. However, questions remain about whether the reduced speed seen in the aged is due to: a) a general "speed" factor, which is a reduction in all central nervous system activity (Birren et al., 1979); b) a deterioration of central mechanisms; or c) a decline in the efficiency of one or more components of the information processing system. It is not known, for example, whether the degree of age-associated slowing depends upon the total amount of central nervous system processing required in a given task, or upon the vulnerability of specific processes to the influence of age.

COMPONENTS OF THE
INFORMATION PROCESSING SYSTEM

The current information processing models that describe perceptual and cognitive functions that are active before and during psychomotor performance assume that human processing operates within a limited capacity system (for review, see Schmidt, 1982). Although investigators have only recently begun to study aging effects on isolated components of the system, age-related decrements have been found in most components of the information processing system studied to date: peripheral processing, short-term sensory storage, short-term memory, long-term memory, and motor programming.

Peripheral Processing

Peripheral processing includes stimulus identification, feature extraction, and pattern recognition. Age-related decreases have been seen in perceptual processing when the characteristics of the stimuli have been experimentally manipulated (e.g., intensity, duration, probability of oc-

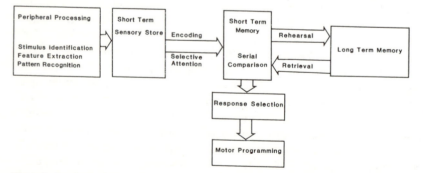

Figure 1. A typical model of human information processing, from receipt of the stimulus to movement execution, modified from Schmidt, R.A., *Motor Control and Learning.* Champaign, IL: Human Kinetics Publ., 1982, p. 115.

currence), signal/noise ratio, information content, and capability of response (Naylor, 1973; Salthouse & Somberg, 1982a; Simon & Pouraghabagher, 1978; Walsh, 1976).

Central Processing

Central processing is a generalized term for sensory storage (STS), short-term memory (STM), encoding processes, long-term memory (LTM), response selection, and response programming. Several investigators have found that central processing, which they defined as one, all, or combinations of these components, is detrimentally affected by aging (Hertzog, 1978; Katzman & Terry, 1983; Kline & Birren, 1975; Kline & Szafran, 1975; Walsh, 1976; Walsh & Thompson, 1978).

Short-Term Sensory Store

The short-term store is proposed to be the most peripheral memory system that accepts, with little if any coding, large amounts of information and holds it for a brief period of time. The contacts made in STS fade quickly; the longer they are held in STS, the more of them may be selectively attended to and coded for later operations in short-term memory. The sensory memory capacity of the aged is less (Schonfield & Wenger, 1975), and the length of time items can be held in memory is shorter. Iconic memory in the young, for example, is 40 msec longer than that of the old. This represents a 12% deficit in the iconic memory of the aged (Walsh & Thompson, 1978).

Encoding to Short-Term Memory (Selective Attention)

Inasmuch as a multitude of stimuli constantly contact the short-term store, some mechanism exists to select the stimuli to be processed while allowing others to dissipate. Those stimuli attended to are coded into short-term memory, and since the system has a limited capacity, those not immediately attended to must wait. The delay noted in an individual's response to the second of two closely spaced stimuli, or the psychological refractory period, is evidence for a limited processing system. The psychological refractory period is disproportionately long in the aged (Botwinick, 1978; Welford, 1977). Old individuals also have more difficulty ignoring irrelevant information; their attention span declines (Hoyer & Plude, 1980). This finding is questioned, however, as Simon and Pouraghabagher (1978) failed to find attention deficits in the elderly. They also suggested that since the elderly were slower in a choice reaction time task when the stimulus was degraded, they do not process stimuli slower but are just slower at the encoding stage.

Short-Term Memory

The capacity of short-term memory—the working space of the memory system—seems little affected by aging, but scanning and comparing item by item is slower as one ages (Birren et al., 1979; Botwinick, 1978; Salthouse & Somberg, 1982a). This has been shown by experiments in which the number of items in the memory set was varied; the old were significantly slower with an increased number of items to remember. Both the slope and the intercept were affected by aging (Anders & Fozard, 1973; Anders, Fozard, & Lillyquist, 1972; Erickson, Hamlin, & Daye, 1973). That is, the overall speed of the old subjects' response was slower (intercept), but the lengthening of response time was relatively greater in the old as the size of the memory set increased (slope).

Another example of the aging effect on short-term memory concerns the performance of the elderly on the Digit Symbol test. This test has been used to calculate coding time (e.g., Storandt, 1976) by comparing the time subjects require to substitute symbols for digits with the time they require to copy the digits directly without a symbol substitution. By assuming that total time = copying time + coding time, and subtracting the copying time from the total time, a period of time representing the coding of the digits to symbols is extracted. This test has been very sensitive to age effects (Weschler, 1958), and Storandt (1976) found that age effects occurred in both coding time and copying time at a ratio of about 50:50.

A persistent question regarding these psychomotor speed tests is whether the aging effects are due to real deficits in speed or are age changes in the speed/accuracy trade-off phenomenon. It has been suggested that older individuals are more cautious and trade speed for accuracy more than the young do (Welford, 1982). Salthouse and Somberg 1982b) have taken a fresh approach to this question by defining the time-accuracy-operating characteristics of young and old. Using a choice reaction time paradigm, the subjects are given intervals of time in which to make their decisions, progressing from very short to much longer. The dependent variable is the number of correct responses; far fewer correct responses occur in the short intervals than in the longer intervals, where accuracy is almost perfect. In this paradigm, the rate of extracting information is the slope of the regression of accuracy over interval duration. The duration of "all other processes" is provided by the intercept, and a measure of final accuracy is provided by the asymptote. In this model age affected the intercept, or the duration of all other processes, not the rate of information extraction.

This indicates that the elderly need more time to react (intercept), but once given that time their accuracy increases as a function of increased time available in the same manner that it does in young subjects (slope). Given adequately long times in which to respond, the old are also as accurate as the young (asymptote). Furthermore, since young and old adults differ in speed of performance even when being compared at less than perfect levels of accuracy, it is not likely that the age effects can be attributed solely to age differences in accuracy emphasis. In this model, encoding, not serial comparison, is affected by aging.

Response Selection and Programming

The response selection stage of processing is affected by the characteristics of the response to be made: duration, complexity, timing, and rhythm, whether it is a serial, discrete, or continuous response, and whether it requires postural adjustments. Age effects on response selection have not been studied prolifically, but those who have isolated these components have reported deficits in both response selection (Naylor, 1973) and motor programming (Haaland & Bracy III, 1982). Reaction time is affected by response complexity in the old but not in the young; preparation for selection over and above stimulus complexity requires more time in the old (Anders et al., 1972; Griew, 1959; Salthouse & Somberg, 1982b).

Long-Term Memory

Generally, tasks that require repeated sequential processing are most sensitive to age (Botwinick & Thompson, 1968). However, Hulicka (1966) has suggested that if old subjects are allowed to memorize word sets to the same criterion regardless of the number of trials, they remember as much one week later as young subjects do.

PLASTICITY OF THE AGING MOTOR SYSTEM

How malleable is the aging central nervous system? Can some or all of these aging effects be postponed or avoided altogether? Some aging effects can be postponed; others can't (Fries & Crapo, 1981). Some unchangeable effects of aging are arterial wall rigidity, cataract formation, graying of hair, thinning of hair, kidney reserve, and elasticity of skin. Many effects of aging are modifiable, however. For example, some aging effects on skin can be postponed by avoiding sun exposure. Osteoporosis, or bone loss, can be modified by diet and exercise. Intelligence and sociability can be maintained by practice (Fries & Crapo, 1981). Many effects of aging such as physical endurance, cardiac reserve, pulmonary reserve, physical strength, serum cholesterol, and systolic blood pressure can be affected by exercise. These particular aging effects that are modifiable by exercise are also related to psychomotor speed.

Reaction time, for example, is slowest in the cerebrovascular diseased, in patients who have transient ischemic attacks and strokes (Speith, 1965). It is next slowest in brain damaged (Benton, 1977; Hicks & Birren, 1970; Light, 1978; Miller, 1970) and untreated hypertensive patients (Speith, 1965). Birren, Woods, and Williams (1979) suggested that increased sympathetic activity from hypertension may lead to relative inhibition of the CNS with regard to facilitating perceptual and motor responses. Reaction time is also slower than normal in those with coronary heart disease (Botwinick & Storandt, 1974; Hertzog, Schaie, & Gribbin, 1978; Speith, 1964, 1965). In fact, Ferris, Crook, Sathananthan, and Gershon (1976) reported that disjunctive reaction time predicts disease-related mental decline with 86% accuracy. Both hand and foot reaction time are significant factors in the biological age test battery developed by Borkin and Norris (1980). In their longitudinal study, the hand and foot reaction times that were obtained at an earlier date were significantly faster in the surviving group when compared to a deceased group of subjects. Tapping speed was also slower in those with cardiovascular disease and hypertension (Enzer, Simonson, & Blankenstein, 1942).

The hypothesis that exercise may prevent premature aging of the central nervous system, perhaps via modifications of the cardiovascular system or neuroendocrine system, is supported by the observation that psychomotor speed is faster in healthy, physically active individuals when compared to the speed of sedentary individuals. Numerous investigators have found that people who exercise consistently are faster in measures of simple and choice reaction time (Hart, 1981; Sherwood & Selder, 1979; Spirduso, 1975; Spirduso & Clifford, 1978). These studies show that the reactive speed of the fingers or hands is faster in persons who exercise by running; that is, the response of an unexercised finger or hand is faster in individuals who primarily exercise their legs. In fact, neither the simple reaction time, choice reaction time, nor hand movement time was faster in racquetball players (persons who exercise their hands and arms as well as their legs) than in runners (Spirduso & Clifford, 1978). This would indicate that the exercise effect on reactivity is a central effect that operates predominantly on the information processing system, and to a lesser extent on the muscle characteristics.

While the evidence is persuasive that differences in information processing exist between physically active and sedentary individuals, the locus of the effect is far from clear. Some investigators have used the subtraction method in attempting to isolate these effects.

Teräväinen and Calne (1982) computed an "index of processing time" by recalculating data from recent studies (Clarkson, 1978; Spirduso, 1975; Spirduso & Clifford, 1978). In order to determine whether physical activity affects processing time, they subtracted simple reaction time from choice reaction time in both young and old groups and then calculated the degree of difference among the groups based on age and physical fitness level. Their conclusion was that physical activity has no effect on processing time, but rather on motor speed. The index, however, rather than failing to support an effect of physical activity on processing time, provides indirect information as to where the effect of exercise might occur within the information processing model.

The index of processing calculated by Teräväinen & Calne (1982) leads to the surprising conclusion that old active individuals take considerably longer to process information than old inactive and young subjects. In fact, these subtractions indicated that active individuals of any age were slower at processing than were inactive individuals. There also were no age differences in processing time! This seems remarkable, since age differences in processing time are commonly reported, and processing time as measured by electromyographically fractionated reaction time has always been slower in inactive individuals and slower in aged individuals (Clarkson, 1978; Hart, 1981).

The basis for this apparent contradiction appears to be in the interpretation of an index obtained by subtraction, as a measure of information processing time. The index is, rather, a measure of the additional processing time that individuals take to make a choice. It represents only 8-21% of the actual reaction time, whereas information processing comprises from 62-69% of the reaction (Clarkson, 1978; Hart, 1981), depending upon characteristics of the instrument used to acquire the reactions. What Teräväinen & Calne (1982) have revealed is that simple reaction time in Spirduso's (1975) study was substantially faster in active than in inactive individuals, and while choice reaction time was also faster, the difference was not as dramatic. Consequently, the difference between simple and choice reaction time is greater in active than in inactive persons. In fractionated paradigms, where both processing time and muscle contractile time are measured by electromyography, no differences were found when the premotor latencies of the simple reaction time condition were subtracted from the choice reaction time premotor latencies. The fact remains, however, that the absolute value of the processing time in active persons is considerably faster than that of inactive persons.

The subtractive index of the additional time needed to make a choice would suggest that the locus of exercise effects must be other than the serial comparison process that occurs in short-term memory. Rather, these effects must occur prior to that in the peripheral stage, short-term store, or in encoding or selective attention mechanisms. Since older individuals are slower in short-term sensory store (Walsh & Thompson, 1978), slower at encoding a degraded stimulus (Simon & Pouraghabagher, 1978), and have less sensory memory capacity (Schonfield & Wenger, 1975), there is ample evidence that these are sites where

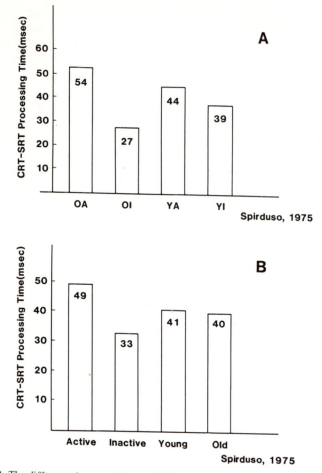

Figure 2. The difference in msec between choice reaction time (CRT) and simple reaction time (SRT). In A, the SRT values reported by Spirduso (1975) for each activity-age group were subtracted from their CRTs. Thus, the difference between the Old Active (OA) subjects' CRT and SRT was 54 msec; the Old Inactive (OI), 27 msec; Young Active (YA) 44 msec; and Young Inactive, 39 msec.

In B, the CRT-SRT differences are averaged across age groups, Active CRT-SRT = 49 msec; Inactive CRT-SRT; 33 msec, and across activity levels, Young CRT-SRT = 41 msec, and Old, CRT-SRT = 40 msec.

physiological effects of exercise might exert modifications. One should also remember that Salthouse and Somberg (1982b) found that aging affects all processes other than that in which information is extracted; that is, aging did not, in their paradigm, have deleterious effects on subjects' abilities to process the additional bits of information provided in the choice reaction time paradigm. On this basis, it seems reasonable to propose that physical fitness does not influence a short-term memory operation that may not even be degraded by aging.

These considerations support the notion that chronic exercise does not affect all levels or stages of information processing, and argue against the notion of a generalized central nervous system slowing (Birren et al., 1979). The possibility that active individuals have a higher arousal level that can be maintained at a higher level is not ruled out (deVries, 1970). Researchers have not yet had the techniques necessary to isolate specific processes that might be modified by exercise, but great progress is being made. It does appear that "some efficient integration of autonomic activity with speed of behavior appears to exist in well-functioning individuals" (Batkin, Note 1). Exercise seems to be one way for people to achieve maximal plasticity in aging, approximating full vigor and consistency of performance until life's end. As such, exercise should be pursued by everyone, inasmuch as psychomotor tasks represent a multitude of small motor tasks that have great significance in everyday life.

REFERENCE NOTE

1. Batkin S. *Aging and the nervous system*. Communication to the XIII International Congress of Gerontology, Hamburg, 1981.

REFERENCES

ANDERS, T.R., & Fozard, J.L. Effects of age upon retrieval from primary and secondary memory. *Developmental Psychology*, 1973, **9**, 411-415.

ANDERS, T.R., Fozard, J.L., & Lillyquist, T.D. Effects of age upon retrieval from short-term memory. *Developmental Psychology*, 1972, **6**, 214-217.

BENTON, A.L. Interactive effects of age and brain disease on reaction time. *Archives of Neurology*, 1977, **34**, 369-370.

BIRREN, J.E., Woods, A.M., & Williams, M.V. Speed of behavior as an indicator of age changes and the integrity of the nervous system. In F. Hoffmeister & C. Muller (Eds.), *Brain function in old age*. Berlin: Springer-Verlag, 1979.

BORKIN, G.A., & Norris, A.H. Assessment of biological age using a profile of physical parameters. *Journal of Gerontology*, 1980, **35**, 177-184.

BOTWINICK, J. *Aging and behavior* (2nd ed.), New York: Springer, 1978.

BOTWINICK, J., & Storandt, M. Speed functions, vocabulary ability and age. *Perceptual Motor Skills*, 1973, **36**, 1128.

BOTWINICK, J., & Thompson, L.W. Age differences in reaction time: An artifact? *Gerontologist*, 1968, **8**, 25-28.

CERELLA, J., Poon, L.W., & Williams, D.M. Age and the complexity hypothesis. In L.W. Poon (Ed.), *Aging in the 1980's*. Washington, DC: American Psychological Association, 1980.

CLARKSON, P.M. The effect of age and physical activity level on simple and choice fractionated response time. *European Journal of Applied Physiology*, 1978, **40**, 17-25.

deVRIES, H.A. Physiological effects of an exercise training regimen upon men 52 to 88. *Journal of Gerontology*, 1970, **25**, 325-336.

ENZER, N., Simonson, E., & Blankenstein, S.S. Fatigue of patients with circulatory insufficiency, investigated by means of fusion frequency of flicker. *Annals of Internal Medicine*, 1942, **16**, 701-707.

ERICKSON, C.W., Hamlin, R.M., & Daye, C. Aging adults and rate of memory scan. *Bulletin of the Psychonomics Society*, 1973, **1**, 259-260.

FERRIS, S., Crook, T., Sathananthan, G., & Gershon, S. Reaction time as a diagnostic measure in senility. *Journal of the American Geriatrics Society*, 1976, **24**, 529-533.

FRIES, J.F., & Crapo, L.M. *Vitality and aging*. San Francisco: W.H. Freeman, 1981.

GRIEW, S. Complexity of response and time of initiating responses in relation to age. *American Journal of Psychology*, 1959, **72**, 83-88.

HAALAND, K.Y., & Bracy III, O.L. Premotor potentials: Implications for the aging motor system. In J.A. Mortimer, F.J. Pirozzolo, & G.J. Maletta (Eds.), *The aging motor system*. New York: Praeger Scientific, 1982.

HART, B.A. The effect of age and habitual activity on the fractionated components of resisted and unresisted response time. *Medicine and Science in Sports and Exercise*, 1981, **13**, 78.

HERTZOG, C., Schaie, K.W., & Gribbin, K. Cardiovascular disease and changes in intellectual functioning from middle to old age. *Journal of Gerontology*, 1978, **33**, 872-883.

HICKS, L.H., & Birren, J.E. Aging, brain damage, and psychomotor slowing. *Psychological Bulletin*, 1970, **74**, 377-396.

HOYER, W.J., & Plude, D.J. Attentional and perceptual processes in the study of cognitive aging. In L.W. Poon (Ed.), *Aging in the 1980's*. Washington, DC: American Psychological Association, 1980.

HULICKA, I.M. Age differences in Wechsler memory scale scores. *Journal of General Psychology*, 1966, **109**, 135.

KATZMAN, R., & Terry, R. Normal aging of the nervous system. In R. Katzman & R. Terry (Eds.), *The neurology of aging*. Philadelphia: F.A. Davis, 1982.

KLINE, R.L., & Birren, J.E. Age differences in backward dicoptic masking. *Experimental Aging Research*, 1975, **1**, 17-25.

KLINE, D.W., & Szafran, J. Age differences in backward monoptic visual noise masking. *Journal of Gerontology*, 1975, **30**, 307.

LIGHT, K. Effects of mild cardiovascular and cerebrovascular disorders on serial reaction time performance. *Experimental Aging Research*, 1978, **4**, 3-22.

MILLER, E. Simple and choice reaction time following severe head injury. *Cortex*, 1970, **6**, 121-127.

NAYLOR, G.F.K. The anatomy of reaction time and its relation to mental function in the elderly. *Proceedings of the Australian Association of Gerontology*, 1973, **2**, 17-19.

RABBITT, P., & Rogers, M. Age and choice between responses in a self-paced repetitive task. *Ergonomics*, 1965, **8**, 435-444.

SALTHOUSE, T.A., & Somberg, B.L. Isolating the age deficit in speeded performance. *Journal of Gerontology*, 1982, **37**, 59-63. (a)

SALTHOUSE, T.A., & Somberg, B.L. Time-accuracy relationships in young and old adults. *Journal of Gerontology*, 1982, **37**, 349-353. (b)

SCHMIDT, R.A. *Motor control and learning.* Champaign, IL: Human Kinetics, 1982.

SCHONFIELD, D., & Wenger, L. Age limit of perceptual span. *Science*, 1975, **253**, 377-378.

SHERWOOD, D.E., & Selder, D.J. Cardiovascular health, reaction time, and aging. *Medicine and Science in Exercise and Sport*, 1979, **11**, 186-189.

SIMON, J.R., & Pouraghabagher, A.R. The effect of aging on the stages of processing in a choice reaction time task. *Journal of Gerontology*, 1978, **33**, 553-561.

SPEITH, W. Cardiovascular health status, age, and psychological performance. *Journal of Gerontology*, 1964, **19**, 277-284.

SPEITH, W. Slowness of task performance and cardiovascular diseases. In A.R. Welford & J.E. Birren (Eds.), *Behavior, aging and the nervous system*. Springfield, IL: Charles C. Thomas, 1965.

SPIRDUSO, W.W. Reaction and movement time as a function of age and physical activity level. *Journal of Gerontology*, 1975, **30**, 435.

SPIRDUSO, W.W., & Clifford, P. Replication of age and physical activity effects on reaction and movement time. *Journal of Gerontology*, 1978, **33**, 26-30.

STORANDT, M. Speed and coding effects in relation to age and ability level. *Developmental Psychology*, 1976, **12**, 177-178.

TERÄVÄINEN, H., & Calne, D.B. Motor system in normal aging and Parkinson's disease. In R. Katzman & R. Terry (Eds.), *Neurology of aging*. Philadelphia: F.A. Davis, 1982.

WALSH, D.A. Age differences in central perceptual processing: A dichoptic backward masking investigation. *Journal of Gerontology*, 1976, **31**, 178.

WALSH, D.A., & Thompson, L.W. Age differences in visual sensory memory. *Journal of Gerontology*, 1978, **33**, 383-387.

WEISS, A.D. The locus of reaction time change with set, motivation, and age. *Journal of Gerontology*, 1965, **20**, 60-64.

WELFORD, A.T. Serial reaction times, continuity of task, single-channel effects, and age. In S. Dornic (Ed.), *Attention and performance* VI. Hillsdale, NJ: Lawrence Erlbaum, 1977.

WELFORD, A.T. Motor skills and aging. In J.A. Mortimer, F.J. Pirozzolo, & G.J. Maletta (Eds.), *The aging motor system*. New York: Praeger Scientific, 1982.

WESCHLER, D. *The measurement and appraisal of adult intelligence*. Baltimore: Williams & Wilkins, 1958.

The Longevity, Morbidity, and Physical Fitness of Former Athletes—An Update

K.E. Stephens, W.D. Van Huss,
H.W. Olson, and H.J. Montoye
Michigan State University

The effects of intensive athletic competition have long been a subject of interest. The 19th century viewpoint was that athletic competition reduced longevity (Hartley & Llewellyn, 1939), but this has been refuted consistently in most subsequent studies. This paper will briefly review, update, and summarize the evidence in the various lines of investigation: a) the athlete-longevity studies in which comparisons were made with population data, b) the athlete-longevity studies in which the comparisons were made with control groups, and c) the studies in which quantitative data were collected on older athletes. Additional information will also be presented, such as the effects of athletic participation upon mortality and the relationship between activity level in 1960 to subsequent mortality.

ATHLETE LONGEVITY STUDIES

Comparison With Population Data

Table 1 summarizes 17 athlete-population studies. Findings from 16 of them favor a lower athlete mortality, whether expressed in additional years of life or mortality ratio, and the remaining study (Pomeroy & White, 1958) had nonspecified findings. It is clear from the consistent findings that athletes live longer than other individuals.

While the more recent studies (Karvonen, Klemola, Virkajarvi, & Kekkonen, 1974; Metropolitan Life, 1975; Pyorala, Karvonen, Taskinen, Takkunen, Kyronseppa, & Peltokallio, 1967; Schnohr, 1971) have added to the body of data, two specifically (Schnohr, 1971, 1972; Metropolitan Life, 1975) have suggested that caliber of athlete or level of competition influences longevity. Their respective elite performers were

Table 1

Summary of Athlete Longevity Studies: Comparisons with Population Data

Investigator	Year	Examined population	Number	Comparison population	Findings	Comments
Morgan	1873	1829-1859 Oxford and Cambridge University oarsmen	251	Dr. Farr's English Life Tables	Athletes favored	By 2.0 years
Meylan	1904	1852-1892 Harvard University oarsmen	152	Standard mortality tables	Athletes favored	By 2.88 years
Gaines and Hunter	1906	Pre 1905 Yale University athletes	Unspecified	Insurance tables	Athletes favored	Mortality ratio 49%
Anderson	1916	1855-1905 Yale University athletes	808	Actuarial Society Table (AST) and American Table (AT)	Athletes favored	AST mortality ratio 52% AT mortality ratio 46%
Hill	1927	1800-1888 British cricket players	3,424	English Life Table No. 4 and English Life Table No. 8	Athletes favored	Significant at all ages, all comparisons
Dublin	1928	1890-1905 athletes from 10 eastern American colleges	4,976	Medico-Actuarial Table (MA) and American Men Table of Mortality (AMTM)	Athletes favored	MA mortality ratio 93.2% AMTM mortality ratio 91.5%
Reed and Love	1931	1901 (in service) - 1916 (commissioned before) West Point Military Academy officers	Unspecified (Total Study N = 4,991)	American Men Table of Mortality and West Point officers	Athletes favored	By .25-1.25 years
Cooper, O'Sullivan and Hughes	1937	Ormand College (Australia oarsmen)	100	Australian Insurance Table (AIT)	Athletes favored	Mortality ratio 75.4%

	Year	Population	n	Comparison group	Result	Findings
Hartley and Llewellyn	1939	1829-1928 Oxford and Cambridge University oarsmen	767	4 standard mortality tables (Hm, Qm, X_{o_m} + A, A)	Athletes favored	Period 1 mortality ratio 87.8%; Period 2 mortality ratio 76.7%; Period 3 mortality ratio 85.1%; Period 4 mortality ratio 93.5%
Wakefield	1944	1911-1935 Indiana high school basketball players	2,919	United States Bureau of Census life tables	Athletes favored	Mortality ratio 67.9%
Schmid	1952	1861-1800 Czechoslovakian athletes	400	General population nonathletes	Athletes favored	By 8.66-1.44 years
Pomeroy and White	1958	1900-1930 Harvard University football lettermen	424	1940 general Massachusetts population and other Harvard graduates	Unspecified	Athlete-population comparison not possible; coronary group engaged in less vigorous and habitual exercise
Karvonen	1959	Pre 1930 Finnish champion skiers	388	1931-1940 and 1951-1955 general male Finnish population and 1949-1953 insurance population	Athletes favored	By 6-7 years over 1931-1940; smaller differences over 1951-1953; nonsignificant differences with insurance population
Pyorala et al.	1967	Finnish long distance runners and skiers	93	Randomly selected Finnish population	Athletes favored	Have a higher degree of activity; mortality ratio-comparison not made.
Schnohr	1971 1972	1880-1910 Danish champion athletes	297	General male population	Athletes favored	Mortality ratio to age 50, 61%; mortality ratio post age 50, 108-109%
Karvonen et al.	1974	Finnish champion skiers born 1845-1910	396	General male population	Athletes favored	By 3-4 years
Metropolitan Life	1975	1876-1973 major league baseball players	6,753	General population (white males) of the United States	Athletes favored	1876-1900 mortality ratio 103% 1901-1973 mortality ratio 71%

shown to have a substantially lower mortality than the general population.

Comparisons with actuarial-life tables, however, have been criticized. College athletes, especially those of the early investigations, are a select group by virtue of their attendance at a university. Elite amateur performers (Schnohr, 1971, 1972) and professional athletes (Metropolitan Life, 1975) are also select groups because of their exceptional athletic prowess. To get at the basic question of whether the athletic participation has affected the longevity and morbidity, adequate controls are needed.

Comparisons With Control Groups

Table 2 summarizes the studies involving control groups. Results from investigations using university classmates as control groups are not consistent. In some instances the controls were favored (Greenway & Hiscock, 1926); in two there was no difference (Montoye, Van Huss, Pierson, Olson, & Hudec, 1957; Rook, 1954); in others the athletes were favored (Paffenbarger, Natkin, Krueger et al., 1966; Paffenbarger & Wing, 1967; Prout, 1972). Polednak and Damon (1970) and Polednak (1972a, b, & c) have found minor athletes and nonathletes favored over the major athletes. Honors men appear to have a greater longevity than either athletes or nonathletes in school at the same time. The results of these studies, however, are inconsistent and confusing.

Furthermore, there is a need to institute some new investigations. The amount of training required to excel today is far greater than it was several decades ago. It is not uncommon for age-group swimmers to train at 10-13,000 yards a day or for distance runners to cover 120-160 miles a week. The female high school swimmers today are achieving what were male Olympic times in the 1940s. The data from current longevity-morbidity studies of athletes are clearly not applicable.

There is also a need to control for the differences in the physiological-anatomical adaptations of the diverse types of fitness required for different sports. The long-range effects of most of these highly specific fitnesses are not known. A further examination of such effects requires information on both exercise and control groups concerning body build, type of sport fitness, and the current activity level. The optimal study is longitudinal with repeated measures.

The longevity-of-athlete data have been criticized by Sheehan (1972, 1973) because the studies to date have not controlled for somatotype. It is his point that the differences observed by Prout (1972), Schnohr (1971, 1972), Largey (1972), Polednak (1972), and others are simply a tendency of specific populations to have different body builds. Since studies on the general population have shown that certain somatotypes, such as the endomesomorphic types so well adapted to line play in

Table 2

Summary of Athlete Longevity Studies: Comparisons with Control Groups

Investigator	Year	Examined population	Number	Comparison population	Number	Findings	Comments
Greenway and Hiscock	1926	Post 1904 Yale University lettermen	686	1905-1923 Yale University nonlettermen	9,421	Controls favored controls 83%; "Y" men 93%	Actual to expected deaths (%);
Dublin	1932	1870-1905 eastern American college lettermen	4,976	1870-1905 eastern American college (8) nonlettermen	38,269	Honors men (controls) favored	Generally by 2 years—over both athletes and other students (nonsignificant)
Rook	1941	1860-1900 Cambridge University athletes	772	1860-1900 Cambridge University honors and random graduates	374 (honors) 336 (random)	Honors men (controls) favored; random group (controls) no difference	Honors men by 1.5 years—over both athletes and other students
Montoye et al.	1957	Pre 1938 Michigan State University lettermen	628	Pre 1938 Michigan State University students	563 563	No difference (in age at death)	122 deceased
Montoye et al.	1962	Pre 1938 Michigan State University lettermen	628	Pre 1938 Michigan State University students	563	No difference (in age at death)	206 deceased
Montoye	1967	Pre 1938 Michigan State University lettermen	628	Pre 1938 Michigan State University students	563	Nonathletes favored	By 2 years (nonsignificant)

Table 2 (Cont.)

Author	Year		N		N		
Paffenbarger et al.	1966	1921-1950 University of Pennsylvania and Harvard University varsity athletes	63	1921-1950 University of Pennsylvania and Harvard University students	590	Athletes favored (in coronary heart deaths)	Mortality ratio = .6
Paffenbarger et al.	1967	1921-1950 University of Pennsylvania and Harvard University varsity athletes	118	1921-1950 University of Pennsylvania and Harvard University students	855	Athletes favored (in fatal stroke)	Mortality ratio = .4
Polednak and Damon	1970	1880-1916 Harvard University lettermen (major athletes)	177	1880-1916 Harvard University students (minor and nonathletes)	275 (minor) 1638 (non)	Minor athletes favored	Major athletes shortest lived
Polednak	1972a 1972b 1972c	1880-1916 Harvard University lettermen (major athletes)	668	1880-1916 Harvard University students (minor and nonathletes)	1501 (minor) 4134 (non)	Minor athletes and nonathletes favored	By 1-3 years
Olson et al.	1972	Pre 1938 Michigan State University lettermen	628	Pre 1938 Michigan State University students	563	Nonathletes favored	By 1.4 years (nonsignificant)
Prout	1972	1882-1902 Harvard and Yale University crews	172	1882-1902 Harvard and Yale University students	172	Athletes favored	By 6.24-6.35 years (significant)
Olson et al.	1978	Pre 1938 Michigan State University lettermen	628	Pre 1938 Michigan State University students	563	Nonathletes favored	By 1.86 years (nonsignificant)

football, have a shorter life span (Spain, Nathan, & Gelles, 1963), there is a need to control for somatotype. In reviewing "Who Was Who in American Sports," Largey (1972) observed that the trackmen's longevity was 14 years longer than that of football players. Clearly, future studies must consider somatotype if we are to assess adequately the long-range effects of athletic participation.

The studies summarized in Table 2 that have been published since 1970, in particular, have pointed to the need for control of body build. The Polednak and Damon (1970), Polednak (1972a, b, & c), Olson (1972), and Olson, Montoye, Sprague, Stephens, and Van Huss (1978) studies reflect this need. The greater longevity of the minor athletes in the Polednak data is also evident in the progressive increase in mortality in the athlete data of the Michigan State study as presented by Montoye and associates (1957, 1962, 1967) and by Olson et al. (1972, 1978). This trend is likely related to body type. In 1973 the percent deceased was 43.7 for the athletes and 40.9 for the nonathletes ($P = 0.35$); the age at death was 68.18 years for the athletes and 70.22 for the nonathletes ($P = 0.21$); the percentage dying of cardiovascular disease was 22.1 for the athletes and 19.1 for the nonathletes; the athlete-nonathlete comparisons, grouping the major causes of death into cancer, cardiovascular, and other, were not significant ($P = 0.52$). Preliminary work indicates that since the in-college heights and weights are available, and the weight changes and current weights have been obtained at each 7-year follow-up, one may arrive at a gross body-build classification by matching the weight gain patterns to those presented by Sheldon and Dupertuis (1954). This is the next step in the Michigan State study in addition to collecting the next follow-up data in 1983-84.

Two subitems merit mention: the effect of the number of years of sports participation upon mortality in college athletes, and the effects of vocational and avocational activity levels on the longevity of athletes and nonathletes.

Years of Sports Participation and Mortality. This study was conducted using the Michigan State data (Olson, Teitelbaum, Van Huss, & Montoye, 1977). The mean years of sports participation for the living and deceased athletes and nonathletes are shown in Table 3. The years of sports participation for the athletes was significantly greater, as would be expected. When the years of sports participation of the subjects surviving in 1968 were compared with the years of sports participation of those deceased between 1952 and 1968, no significant differences were observed in the combined groups or in either the athlete or nonathlete groups. The mean years of sports participation were slightly less for both the deceased athletes and nonathletes as compared to their living counterparts. The significant status × time interaction for the nonathletes should be discounted because it was produced by an abnormally high value (11.2

Table 3

Mean Years of Sports Participation

Subjects	N	Years of participation
Athlete living	442	7.81
Athlete deceased	113	6.89
Nonathlete living	417	4.02
Nonathlete deceased	87	3.74

Analysis of variance

Comparison	F-value	Probability
Athlete vs nonathlete	85.01	.001
Living vs deceased (status)	1.55	.213
Date of birth (time)	2.19	.113
Status × time	7.92	.402
Athlete group:		
Living vs deceased	1.91	.168
Status × time	0.76	.467
Nonathlete group:		
Living vs deceased	0.12	.724
Status × time	3.92	.021

years) for the 1875-1879 birthdate data based on only five cases. Across the years of birth no differences in pattern were evident in the living-deceased comparison.

The number of years of sports participation does not seem to have been deleterious in terms of the participants' longevity. The fact that the results favor more years of sports participation among the surviving subjects strengthens the conclusion that the years of sports participation has not materially affected the longevity of the participants.

The Effects of Activity Levels on the Longevity of Athletes and Nonathletes. This study (Stephens, 1978) was based on the Michigan State data. It considered only those respondents in the 1960 follow-up who returned a questionnaire in 1976 or for whom a death certificate was obtained. Selection of this group gave access to both the vocational and avocational data on the 1960 questionnaire. In addition, during the 16-year interval between the 1960 and 1976 studies 155 athletes and 140 nonathletes had died. The resulting data were analyzed for mortality and age at death versus activity pattern comparisons.

Two activity types were drawn from the data and a third—Total Activity—was created by summing the other two: a) The vocational activity pattern utilized the U.S. Employment Service *Dictionary of Occupational Titles* for the classification of occupations, scaled on the basis of retired, sedentary, light, medium, and heavy activity and insufficient data; b) the avocational activity pattern ratings were structured to parallel that for vocational activity patterns. The avocational activity ratings were based on the evaluation of variables on the 1960 questionnaire that included yard and house maintenance, calisthenics, hobbies, and recreational participation. Independent, blind, subjective analyses were made by three investigators. Following the independent ratings the three discussed each case to arrive at a consensus. The following scale was implemented in rating each subject:

- *Sedentary:* one who did minimal yard and house maintenance, participated in a low energy hobby, or walked less than a mile a day;
- *Light:* one who did regular house and yard maintenance or regular calisthenics, had hobbies, participated in seasonal activities, or walked more than one mile a day;
- *Medium:* one who did regular house and yard maintenance, had hobbies, participated in regular calisthenics including rhythmical endurance exercises, and regularly participated in a low energy sport such as golf;
- *Heavy:* an individual was considered to have a heavy activity if he or she participated in all four above activities regularly or if a high energy sport or activity was part of his or her regular pattern.

The total activity levels combined the vocational and avocational ratings. The initial category consisted of these subjects who were sedentary avocationally and either sedentary or retired vocationally. Category 2 was a relative measure of those who were not sedentary, including those avocationally sedentary and vocationally light or those avocationally light and vocationally sedentary or retired. Category 3 included the remaining subjects, those individuals who participated in significantly more activity than either the sedentary or light activity subjects. The activity levels were not high enough to include a fourth category. While not an absolute measure of activity, the categorizations enable comparisons of subjects with a progressive increase in activity levels.

The comparisons of the athlete-nonathlete results are shown in Figure 1. None of the differences were statistically significant. In the subsequent analyses shown in Figure 2 the athlete-nonathlete comparison is disregarded and the total data pooled. In these comparisons, which are blocked by data of birth groupings, the subjects deceased between 1960 and 1976 are compared on the basis of their respective activity levels reported in 1960. Due to the subjective nature of the ratings, an alpha level of .10 was used for these analyses.

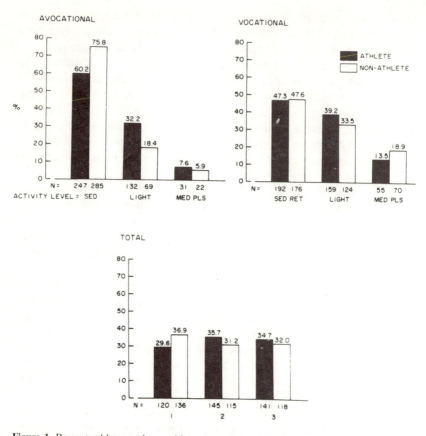

Figure 1. Percent athletes and nonathletes in varied activity levels.

Across the three activity levels as reported in 1960, the sedentary group had a significantly greater number deceased in the 1880-1889 grouping than for the light and medium activity levels. The same trend holds across the 1890-1899 vocational and avocational ratings but not for the totals. The 1900-1909 grouping is difficult because significantly more with the avocational-sedentary rating were deceased. For this grouping the vocational and total activity levels were reversed. The 1910-1919 block also differs in that significantly more of the light activity group were deceased between 1960 and 1976.

In summary, these data indicate there was no sharp effect on total activity of impending death between 1960 and 1976 which was evident in 1960. Avocationally a trend indicated that a higher percentage of those most sedentary in 1960 were deceased. Vocationally, in the older age groups those most active in 1960 appeared to have a smaller percentage deceased between 1960 and 1976.

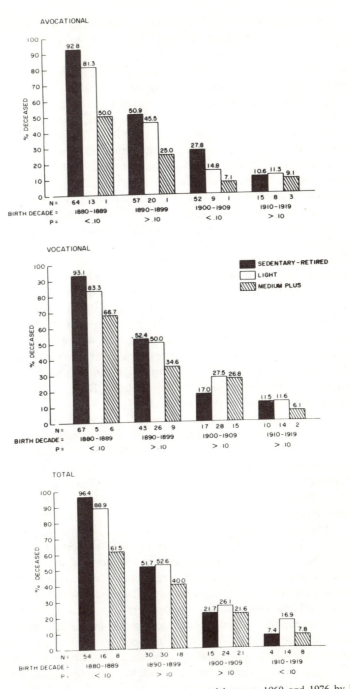

Figure 2. Activity level in 1960 and percent deceased between 1960 and 1976 by birth decade.

QUANTITATIVE MEASURES OF FORMER ATHLETES
AND OLDER ATHLETES STILL ACTIVE

The more recent studies in which quantitative cardiovascular measures have been collected on former athletes who were active or sedentary, and on older athletes still competing, are shown in Table 4. The studies involving the distance performers (i.e., runners, skiers, and cyclists) showed that at rest the former athletes cannot be distinguished from non-athletes if they have not continued to be active. Saltin and Grimby (1968) found that the maximum oxygen consumption of the former runners and skiers was 20% higher than for sedentary middle-aged men, but 25% lower than for still active athletes of the same age. The higher maximal oxygen consumptions and work capacity of the former athletes as compared with nonathletes is particularly evident in the Scandinavian data (Holmgren & Strandell, 1959; Pyorala et al., 1967; Saltin & Grimby, 1968). Such results might be due to the fact that the former athletes represent a selected group. It is also probable that they have maintained a higher degree of physical fitness than controls from the population. The comprehensive data collected by Dill, Robinson, and Ross (1967) and Robinson, Dill, Robinson, Tzankoff, and Wagner (1976) on 16 champion runners and the data of Fardy, Maresh, Abbott, and Kristiansen (1978b) tends to support the greater capacity in the former athletes. In only two of the Robinson-Dill sample was the maximum oxygen consumption below the average for nonathletes. Both of these men were smokers who were also quite sedentary.

Pollock, Miller, and Wilmore (1974) studied champion masters runners. They observed small decrements in maximum performance and oxygen intake capacity with age up to age 60. The largest reductions were observed after 60 years of age. The body composition, maximum pulmonary ventilations, heart rates, and blood pressures in these still active athletes also held fairly steady up to 65 years but showed a decrement thereafter.

Fardy and associates (Fardy, Maresh, & Abbott, 1976; Fardy, Maresh, Abbott, & Kristiansen, 1978a, 1978b) performed the largest scale study of 350 former athletes and 158 nonathletes in which quantitative laboratory data were collected. He attempted multiple combinations for analysis. No differences were observed between former athletes and nonathletes engaged in strenuous leisure activities. Systolic time intervals were longer, the maximum oxygen consumption higher, and heart rates were consistently lower in the former athletes. However, the former athletes also weighed less and were more active in their leisure time. No differences were observed when the former athlete sample was divided into three categories of sport types, that is, individual, team, and individual plus team. It would be interesting if the data of Fardy and

Table 4

Cardiovascular Characteristics of Former Athletes and Older Athletes Still Active

Investigator	Year	Examined population	Number	Comments and findings
Holmgren and Strandell	1959	Racing cyclists mean age 49.5 yrs post competition	19	Had raced for an average of 12.7 yrs. Measured post competition averaging 18 yrs. Eight of 19 showed pathological ECGs. Heart volume was unchanged but total hemoglobin and work capacity was lower. Six subjects who had continued training showed higher work capacities.
Grimby and Saltin	1966	Distance runners 42-68 yrs still competing	33	Systolic blood pressure same as population but diastolic was lower. No significant difference in oxygen uptake between age groups at standard workloads but the ventilations, heart rates, and lactate levels were higher in the older subjects. The maximum oxygen consumption and heart rates were lower in the older subjects.
Grimby et al.	1966	Distance runners and skiers 45-55 yrs in training for 20 yrs	9	Max stroke volume and heart volumes did not differ from young subjects. Cardiac output values were observed to 30 l/min, a high value for young athletes. Max oxygen consumption was lower than in trained young men but higher than in untrained young men.
Pyorala et al.	1967	Runners (30) and skiers (31) 40-79 yrs	61	All subjects were post competition. Compared with less active, nonathlete controls. Former athletes were more active, hearts were larger. Hypertension was slightly higher in the controls.
Dill et al.	1967	Former champion runners	16	Comprehensive data on each subject. Max oxygen uptake decreased. Those most active retained capacities best. Percent fat was least in those exercising regularly.
Saltin and Grimby	1968	Former athletes sedentary at least 10 yrs 45-70 yrs	29	Max oxygen consumption was 20% higher than for sedentary middle aged men but 25% lower than for still active athletes of the same age. Heart volume was same as the still active athletes. No differences in ECG except in frequency. Stroke volumes compared favorably with young athletes in the trained older group.

Table 4 (Cont.)

Pollock et al.	1974	Champion masters runners	25	Maximum performance and oxygen intake decreased with age, with the largest reductions after 60 yrs of age. Body composition, max pulmonary ventilation, heart rates and blood pressures were similar to age 65 but showed a decrement thereafter.
Fardy et al.	1976	Former athletes and nonathletes 27-74 yrs	350 (Ath) 158 (NA)	No differences observed between former athletes and nonathletes engaged in strenuous leisure activities. Myocardial function of former athletes were superior to former nonathletes of the same age and physical activity habits (below strenuous).
Robinson et al.	1976	Former champion runners 47-68 yrs	16	Former athletes at rest similar to nonathletes. Max VO_2 had declined from 71.4 to 41.8 ml/kg/min at 56.6 yrs. Mean max heart rate declined from 186 to 180 and from 199-186 in nonathletes at corresponding ages.
Fardy et al.	1978a	Former athletes 27-74 yrs	350	The former athletes were divided into three categories according to sport type, i.e., team, individual, or team and individual. No differences in max VO_2, heart rate systolic time intervals, or blood pressures, leisure time activities, or smoking habits.
Fardy et al.	1978b	Former athletes and nonathletes	350 156	Systolic time intervals were longer, max VO_2 higher, and heart rates were consistently lower in the former athletes. Former athletes weighed less, smoked less and were more active in their leisure time than nonathletes.
Heath et al.	1981	Trained masters endurance runners 59 ± 6 yrs	16	16 trained masters endurance athletes were matched with 16 young runners on the basis of training regimens. They were also compared with 9 other untrained and 9 lean untrained. Max VO_2 was about 15% below young runners but at submaximal levels almost identical. Greater left ventricular volume in the older athletes. Max heart rate was 14% lower in the older athletes. The max VO_2 of the masters athletes was 60% higher than the untrained.

associates could also be sorted and analyzed, grouping the former athletes by the physiological capacities required for the sports such as endurance, power, and repeat power.

One of the most interesting studies completed to date is that of Heath, Hagberg, Ehsani, and Holloszy (1981). In this study, 16 highly trained masters endurance athletes (59 ± 6 years) were matched with 16 young male athletes (22 ± 2 years) who were competing for local colleges and athletic clubs. The subjects were matched on the basis of their training regimens. The masters athletes were also compared to 18 middle-aged untrained men. The untrained men were a select group in that they were nonsmokers, did not develop abnormalities during exercise (i.e., ECG, blood pressure), and were able to attain a true, not symptom-limited maximum oxygen uptake. No significant differences existed between the masters and young athletes in height, weight, or percent body fat (< 10%). In the echocardiographic evaluation, no differences in the athlete groups were observed in left ventricular mass, or in the indicators of myocardial contractile function. Only the end diastolic volume index was greater in the masters athletes.

The maximal responses to exercise and the heart rate and systolic blood pressure responses to a standard progressive treadmill test are shown in Table 5. The maximum oxygen consumption and heart rates were significantly lower for the masters athletes. The systolic blood pressure responses to standard submaximal work were consistently higher for the masters athletes but the heart rates were very similar. Surprisingly, there were no differences between the masters and young athletes in maximum ventilation and oxygen pulse.

When the masters athletes were compared with healthy but untrained middle-aged men, the control men displayed smaller hearts, higher pulse rates and blood pressures during submaximal work, and lower maximal oxygen consumption, ventilation, and oxygen pulse capacities. The differences between the trained and untrained were quite large.

In summary, former athletes who have not continued systematic activity appear nonetheless to possess greater capacities for work and oxygen consumption than their sedentary nonathlete counterparts. It may be, however, that these differences are due to the higher leisure activity patterns of the former athletes. All of the studies that assessed activity level have demonstrated that individuals who stay physically active show less measurable deterioration. In fact, in the one study in which even the training program was controlled for, the age differences in the parameters were minimal. They were much less than the active-inactive group differences. Whether the sharp decline in capacity observed by Pollock et al. (1974) after age 60 is age or activity related is still to be determined.

Table 5

Masters Runners vs Young Runners: Maximal and Submaximal Responses[1]

Standard treadmill test (Bruce)

	Heart rate		Systolic blood pressure	
	Masters athletes	Young athletes	Masters athletes	Young athletes
Resting	55 ± 8	59 ± 7	122 ± 22	117 ± 10
Stage #1	84 ± 17	84 ± 12	150 ± 22	138 ± 12
Stage #2	99 ± 18	101 ± 10	164 ± 18	146 ± 12
Stage #3	116 ± 18	125 ± 14	176 ± 21	162 ± 14

Maximal measures

	Masters athletes	Young athletes
Heart rate (bts)	169 ± 11	197 ± 7
Ventilation (at max O_2) (l/min)	129 ± 19	125 ± 17
Max oxygen uptake ($ml \cdot kg^{-1} \cdot min^{-1}$)	58.7 ± 4.3	69.0 ± 2.3
O_2 pulse ($ml \cdot kg^{-1} \cdot beat^{-1}$)	0.35 ± 0.02	0.35 ± 0.01

[1]Data from Heath et al., 1981.

REFERENCES

ANDERSON, W.G. Further studies in the longevity of Yale athletes. *Medical Times*, 1916, **44**, 75.

COOPER, E.L., O'Sullivan, J., & Hughes, E. Athletes and the heart: An electro-cardiographic and cardiologic study of the responses of the healthy and diseased heart to exercise. *Medical Journal of Australia*, 1937, **1**, 569.

DILL, D.B., Robinson, S., & Ross, J.C. A longitudinal study of 16 champion runners. *Journal of Sports Medicine and Physical Fitness*, 1967, **7**, 4-27.

DUBLIN, L.I. College honor men long lived. *Statistical Bulletin — Metropolitan Life*, 1932, **13**, 5-7.

FARDY, P.S., Maresh, C.M., & Abbott, R.D. A comparison of myocardial function in former athletes and non-athletes. *Medicine and Science in Sports*, 1976, **8**, 26-30.

FARDY, P.S., Maresh, C.M., Abbott, R.D., & Kristiansen, T. Cardiovascular function as influenced by type of prior sport participation. *Preventive Medicine*, 1978, **7**, 407-413. (a)

FARDY, P.S., Maresh, C.M., Abbott, R., & Kristiansen, T. A comparison of habitual lifestyle, aerobic power and systolic time intervals in former athletes and nonathletes. *Journal of Sports Medicine and Physical Fitness*, 1978, **18**, 287-299. (b)

FRANK, C.W., Winblatt, E., Shapiro, S., & Sager, R.V. Physical activity as a lethal factor in myocardial infarction among men. *Circulation*, 1966, **34**, 1022.

GREENWAY, J.C., & Hiscock, I.V. Mortality among Yale men. *Yale Alumni Weekly*, 1926, **35**, 1806-1808.

GRIMBY, G., Nilsson, N.J., & Saltin, B. Cardiac output during submaximal and maximal exercise in active middle-aged athletes. *Journal of Applied Physiology*, 1966, **21**, 1150-1156.

GRIMBY, G., & Saltin, B. Physiological analysis of well trained middle-aged and old athletes. *Acta Medica Scandinavica*, 1966, **179**, 513-526.

HARTLEY, P.H.S., & Llewellyn, G.F. The longevity of oarsmen. *British Medical Journal*, 1939, **1**, 657.

HEATH, G.W., Hagberg, J.M., Ehsani, A.A., & Holloszy, J.O. A physiological comparison of younger and older endurance athletes. *Journal of Applied Physiology*, 1981, **51**, 634-640.

HILL, B. Cricket and its relation to the duration of life. *Lancet*, 1927, **2**, 949.

HOLMGREN, A., & Strandell, T. The relationship between heart volume, total hemoglobin and physical working capacity in former athletes. *Acta Medica Scandinavica*, 1959, **163**, 149-160.

JOKL, E. Longevity of athletes. *Physical Educator*, 1944.

KARVONEN, M.J. Sports and longevity. *Advances in Cardiology*, 1976, **18**, 243.

KARVONEN, M.J., Klemola, H., Virkajarvi, J., & Kekkonen, A. Longevity of endurance skiers. *Medicine and Science in Sports*, 1974, **6**, 49.

LARGEY, G. Athletic activity and longevity. *Lancet*, 1972, **2**, 286.

METROPOLITAN Life. Characteristics of major league baseball players. *Statistical Bulletin — Metropolitan Life*, 1975, **56**, 6.

MEYLAN, G.L. Harvard University oarsmen. *Physical Education Review*, 1904, **9**, 552.

MONTOYE, H.J. Participation in athletics. *Canadian Medical Association Journal*, 1967, **96**, 813.

MONTOYE, H.J. Health and longevity of former athletes. In W.R. Johnson & E.R. Buskirk (Eds.), *Science and medicine of exercise in sport* (2nd ed.). New York: Harper & Rowe, 1974.

MONTOYE, H.J., Van Huss, W.D., & Nevai, J.W. Longevity and morbidity of college athletes: A seven year follow-up study. *Journal of Sports Medicine and Physical Fitness*, 1962, **2**, 133.

MONTOYE, H.J., Van Huss, W.D., Pierson, W.R., Olson, H.W., & Hudec, A.L. *Longevity and morbidity of college athletes.* Indianapolis: Phi Epsilon Kappa, 1957.

MORGAN, J.E. Critical enquiry into the after-health of the men who rowed in Oxford and Cambridge boat races from the year 1829-1859. In *Oxford University Oars*. Cited by Harley and Llewellyn, *British Medical Journal*, 1939, **1**, 658.

OLSON, H.W. *A comparison of longevity and morbidity of athletes and non-athletes.* Unpublished doctoral dissertation, Michigan State University, 1972.

OLSON, H.W., Montoye, H.J., Sprague, H., Stephens, K.E., & Van Huss, W.D. The longevity and morbidity of college athletes. *The Physician and Sportsmedicine*, 1978, **6**, 62.

OLSON, H.W., Teitelbaum, H., Van Huss, W.D., & Montoye, H.J. Years of sports participation and mortality in college athletes. *Journal of Sports Medicine and Physical Fitness*, 1977, **17**, 321.

PAFFENBARGER, R.S., Jr., Natkin, J., Krueger, D.E., Wolf, P.A., Thorn, M.C., LeBauer, E.J., & Williams, J.L. Chronic disease in former college students. II. Methods of study and observations on mortality from coronary heart disease. *American Journal of Public Health*, 1966, **56**, 962.

PAFFENBARGER, R.S., Jr., & Wing, A.L. Characteristics in youth predisposing to fatal stroke in later years. *Lancet*, 1967, **1**, 753.

POLEDNAK, A.P. Previous health and longevity of male athletes. *Lancet*, 1972, **2**, 711. (a)

POLEDNAK, A.P. Longevity and cardiovascular mortality among former college athletes. *Circulation*, 1972, **46**, 649. (b)

POLEDNAK, A.P. Longevity and cause of death among Harvard college athletes and their classmates. *Geriatrics*, 1972, **27**, 53. (c)

POLEDNAK, A.P., & Damon, A. College athletics, longevity and cause of death. *Human Biology*, 1970, **42**, 28.

POLLOCK, M.L., Miller, H.S., & Wilmore, J. Physiological characteristics of champion American track athletes 40-75 years of age. *Journal of Gerontology*, 1974, **29**, 645-649.

POMEROY, W.C., & White, P.D. Coronary heart disease in former football players. *Journal of the American Medical Association*, 1958, **167**, 711.

PROUT, C. Life expectancy of college oarsmen. *Journal of the American Medical Association*, 1972, **220**, 1709.

PYORALA, K., Karvonen, M.J., Taskinen, P., Takkunen, J., & Kyronseppa, H. Cardiovascular studies of former endurance athletes. In M.J. Karvonen & A.J. Barry (Eds.), *Physical activity and the heart*. Springfield, IL: Charles Thomas, 1967.

PYORALA, K., Karvonen, M.J., Taskinen, P., Takkunen, J., Kyronseppa, H., & Peltokallio, P. Cardiovascular studies of former endurance skiers. *American Journal of Cardiology*, 1967, **20**, 191.

REED, L.J., & Love, A.G. Longevity of army officers in relation to physical fitness. *The Military Surgeon*, 1931, **69**, 397.

ROBINSON, S., Dill, D.B., Robinson, R.D., Tzankoff, S.P., & Wagner, J.A. Physiological aging of champion runners. *Journal of Applied Physiology*, 1976, **41**, 46-51.

ROOK, A. An investigation into the longevity of Cambridge sportsmen. *British Medical Journal*, 1954, **1**, 773.

SALTIN, B., & Grimby, G. Physiological analysis of middle-aged and old former athletes. Comparison with still active athletes of the same age. *Circulation*, 1968, **38**, 1104-1115.

SCHMID, V.L. Contributions to the study of the causes of death of sportsmen. *Sportarzt und Sportmedizin*, 1967, **10**, 411.

SCHNOHR, P. Longevity and cause of death in male athletic champions. *Lancet*, 1971, **2**, 1364.

SCHNOHR, P. Athletic activity and longevity. *Lancet*, 1972, **2**, 605.

SHEEHAN, G.A. Athletic activity and longevity. *Lancet*, 1972, **2**, 974.

SHEEHAN, G.A. Longevity of athletes. *The American Heart Journal*, 1973, **86**, 425-426.

SHELDON, W.H., Dupertuis, C.W., & McDermott, E. *Atlas of men*. New York: Harper & Row, 1954.

SPAIN, D.M., Nathan, D.F., & Gelles, G. Weight, body type and the prevalence of coronary atherosclerotic heart disease in males. *American Journal of the Medical Sciences*, 1963, **245**, 63.

STEPHENS, K.E. *The effects of activity patterns on the longevity of athletes and nonathletes*. Unpublished master's thesis, East Lansing, MI: 1978.

WAKEFIELD, M.C. A study of mortality among the men who have played in the Indiana High School State Final Basketball Tournaments. *Research Quarterly*, 1944, **15**, 2.

Athletic Amenorrhea: A Review

Barbara L. Drinkwater
University of Washington

The strenuous training regimens associated with endurance sports have numerous positive effects on physiological function. Women, as well as men, benefit from training by increasing their cardiovascular endurance, reducing body fat, and developing muscular strength and endurance. However, the effect of these programs on the reproductive hormones of the female is much more obvious than in the male and has become the subject of some concern among women, their coaches, and their physicians.

The basic anatomical and physiological differences between the sexes have long been used to explain why women shouldn't—or couldn't—participate in the same activities or at the same level of effort as male athletes. One major point of contention has always been the effect of physical activity on reproductive function or possibility of trauma to the reproductive organs. When a number of survey studies (Åstrand, Eriksson, Nylander, Engstrom, Karlberg, Saltin, & Thoren, 1963; Erdelyi, 1962) were published in the 1960s showing that women athletes had less dysmenorrhea, easier labor, and no evidence of serious damage to uterus or breast, most of the concern dissipated. It appeared that women athletes were well on their way toward equal opportunity in the athletic world. Today that picture has become clouded with reports of an increased incidence of menstrual irregularities and delayed menarche among female athletes.

The reaction to these reports of menstrual dysfunction has varied from speculation that exercise per se may not be the causative agent (Shangold, 1982) to the suggestion that the hormonal response is a form of "endocrine conditioning" similar to that seen in the cardiovascular or skeletal system with training (Prior, 1982). For the most part the reaction has been cautious, an interest and concern about the etiology of the phenomenon, but no suggestion that women cease participating in endurance sports or diminish the intensity of their training. The general tenor of most articles dealing with this topic is that the condition appears to be reversible and that there is no evidence to suggest any long-term effects on the reproductive system (Baker, 1981; Rebar & Cumming, 1981). However, there is also the often repeated caveat that long-term prospective studies are needed to be completely assured that the condition is reversible and that there are no deleterious effects on reproductive function (Baker, 1981; Jacobs, 1982; Prior, 1982; Rebar & Cumming, 1981).

While the term menstrual irregularities covers a wide spectrum of problems, the concern of athletes centers on amenorrhea (absence of menses) or oligomenorrhea (infrequent menses) (Shangold, 1982). Amenorrhea may be either "primary," meaning that menses has never occurred, or "secondary," a cessation of menses following a period of normal cycles. Different investigators define secondary amenorrhea in various ways, ranging from 3 consecutive months without a period (Frisch, Wyshak, & Vincent, 1980), to 6-months intervals (Frisch, Gotz-Welbergen, McArthur, Albright, Witsch, Bullen, Birnholz, Reed, & Herman, 1981; Wakat, Sweeney, & Rogol, 1982) to 10 months with only one period (Shangold & Levine, 1982), or 12 months without menses (Lutter & Cushman, 1982). The basic definition of oligomenorrhea is "infrequent" periods, but infrequent can mean intervals of 38 days to 3 months (Frisch et al., 1980), 36 days or longer (Lutter & Cushman, 1982), 37 days to 6 months (Shangold & Levine, 1982), or cycles that vary $\pm$ 9 days month to month. Since a woman can be classified as amenorrheic in one study and oligomenorrheic in another, acceptance of a standard classification by all investigators would aid in identifying patterns descriptive of each group.

The incidence of oligo/amenorrhea reported in the literature varies widely (Table 1). Part of this variability may reflect how the conditions are defined, but one might also expect the incidence to vary with the population studied. The primary research tool has been the retrospective questionnaire. The respondents varied from women who jog 1 to 5 miles a week (Speroff & Redwine, 1980) to 1,841 entrants in the New York City Marathon (Shangold & Levine, 1982) and professional ballerinas (Cohen, Kim, May, & Ertel, 1982). They ranged in age from the prepubertal to postmenopausal years (Frisch et al., 1980; Speroff & Redwine, 1980). Nevertheless, it is obvious that the incidence of oligo/amenorrhea among these athletes far exceeds the population norm of 2-3%. Nor is the phenomenon limited to running. Swimming, cycling, crew, ballet and other activities involving strenuous physical activity all have a higher than average number of oligo/amenorrhea participants (Baker, 1981; Erdelyi, 1976).

Investigations into the etiology of this form of menstrual dysfunction have relied primarily on survey data to identify those factors

Table 1

Incidence of Oligo/Amenorrhea Among Women Athletes

Reference	Activity	% Oligo/Amenorrhea	% Combined
Cohen et al., 1982	Ballet	6.6/36.6	43.2
Dale et al., 1979	Running		34.0
	Jogging		23.0
Sanborn et al., 1982	Running		25.7
	Swimming		12.3
	Cycling		12.1
Frisch et al., 1980	Ballet	30.0/15.0	45.0
Lutter & Cushman, 1982	Running	19.4/ 3.4	22.8
Schwartz et al., 1981	Running	4.8/15.4	20.2
Shangold & Levine, 1982	Running	18.0/ 6.0	24.0
Speroff & Redwine, 1980	Running	/ 6.0	
Wilmore, Brown, & Davis, 1977	Running	19.0/23.0	42.0

associated with its occurrence in athletic populations (Dale, Gerlach, & Wilhite, 1979; Feicht, Johnson, Martin, Sparkes, & Wagner, 1978; Frisch et al., 1980; Shangold & Levine, 1982; Speroff & Redwine, 1980; Webb, Millan, & Stottz, 1979). A more direct approach involves laboratory evaluation of hormonal responses to exercise, which may have a direct influence on the functioning of the hypothalamic-pituitary-ovarian axis (Baker, Mathur, Kirk, & Williamson, 1981; Bonen, Ling, MacIntyre, Neil, McGrail, & Belcastro, 1979; Bonen, Belcastro, Ling, & Simpson, 1981; Boyden, Pamenter, Grosso, Stanforth, Rotkis, & Wilmore, 1982; Bullen, Skinner, McArthur, & Carr, 1982; Jurkowski, Jones, Walker, Younglai, & Sutton, 1978; Shangold, Freeman, Thysen, & Gatz, 1979; Shangold, Gatz, & Thysen, 1981; Wakat et al., 1982).

From these studies have emerged three theories to explain the association between strenuous physical exercise and oligo/amenorrhea: decrease in percent body fat, hormonal fluctuations resulting from sustained intense exercise, and psychological stress. To understand how each of these factors might influence the cycle, one must understand the normal pattern of hormonal events that culminates in a monthly menses. The normal menstrual cycle is the result of a complex interplay of hormonal events involving the hypothalamus, the pituitary, and the ovaries (Shangold, 1982). The following brief description is based on an extensive review of the literature by Knobil (1980).

Under normal conditions the arcuate nucleus of the hypothalamus discharges a bolus of gonadotropin-releasing hormone (GnRH) approximately once per hour. This bolus reaches the pituitary via the portal circulation and stimulates the secretion of the gonadotropins, follicle-stimulating hormone (FSH), and luteinizing hormone (LH), in a pulsatile fashion — also at a rate of once per hour. During the follicular phase of the cycle, this constant but low-level gonadotropin secretion stimulates the growth and maturation of the immature follicles in the ovary. Early in the follicular stage, relatively low levels of estradiol (E_2) act as a negative feedback at the pituitary to limit the release of LH while low levels of progesterone encourage the secretion of FSH. As the follicles grow they secrete increasing amounts of estradiol. Once the concentration of estradiol reaches approximately 150 pg/ml and remains at that level for 36 hours, its previous negative effect on the pituitary reverses and becomes positive. The result is the typical mid-cycle LH surge that precedes ovulation by a few hours. An increase in GnRH at the same time suggests that the positive feedback effect of estrogen extends to the hypothalamus (Turgeon, 1980).

Following the LH surge, the follicle ruptures and the ovum enters the oviduct on its way to the uterus. The follicular remains evolve into the corpus luteum and produce large amounts of estradiol and progesterone. Immediately following ovulation the concentration of FSH and LH decrease to the levels in the follicular stage, but the maturation of a new follicle is inhibited by the high level of progesterone. As the corpus luteum regresses, the level of progesterone falls, FSH rises, and follicular growth begins again. If all components of the hypothalamic-pituitary-ovarian axis contribute when and as expected, the follicular phase lasts 14 days, ovulation occurs, there is a 14-day luteal phase, and menses follows.

The very complexity of the system ensures that a variation of the norm in one part of the cycle can have a marked effect on other cycle events. For example, a change in the pulsatile release pattern of GnRH at the hypothalamus may result in failure of the ovarian follicle to mature. There will be no ovulation, no progesterone stimulus to the endometrium, and no menses. Any theory relating exercise to oligo/amenorrhea must demonstrate where and how these cyclic events are altered.

The concept that athletic amenorrhea may be related to a decrease in percent body fat is an outgrowth of the Frisch & Revelle (1970) hypothesis that the onset of menarche depends on a "critical weight." Frisch and her co-workers (Frisch, Revelle, & Cook, 1973; Frisch & McArthur, 1974) later modified the hypothesis to emphasize body composition rather than weight per se as the important factor, suggesting 17% body fat as a requirement for menarche and 22% as the level necessary to maintain a regular cycle. At first glance the theory had considerable "face validity" because distance runners and ballet dancers, who have the highest incidence of oligo/amenorrhea, are lean women. Also, a number of survey studies (Dale et al., 1979; Lutter & Cushman,

1982; Sanborn et al., 1982; Shangold & Levine, 1982; Speroff & Redwine, 1980) have reported either a significant relationship between body weight or composition and oligo/amenorrhea, or have found significant differences in weight, weight loss, or percent body fat between normally cycling women and oligo/amenorrheic athletes.

There are several problems with accepting this theory as the sole explanation for the oligo/amenorrhea associated with exercise. An obvious difficulty arises with the determination of body fat. The technique used by Frisch (1974), predicting body composition by using height and weight to estimate total body water (TBW), has been criticized by Trussell (1978) and Reeves (1979) as an imprecise instrument for predicting fatness. Other investigators have used skinfolds (Baker et al., 1981; Schwartz, Cumming, Riordan, Selye, Yen, & Rebar, 1981; Wakat et al., 1982) or simple body weight (Abraham, Beumont, Fraser, & Llewellyn-Jones, 1982; Feicht et al., 1978; Shangold & Levine, 1982) in making comparisons between eumenorrheic and oligo/amenorrheic women. It is unlikely that any of these studies have presented valid estimates of percent body fat. Of the two studies using hydrostatic weighing to estimate fatness, both found a lower fat weight in the oligo/amenorrheic condition (Boyden et al., 1982; Carlberg & Riedesel, 1979).

A number of studies have also failed to show any relationship between weight and/or body composition and oligo/amenorrhea in athletes. Three studies (Baker et al., 1981; Feicht et al., 1978; Wakat et al., 1982) reported no significant difference in weight or body fat between amenorrheic and regularly cycling runners. If body fat were the deciding factor one would expect active women who become inactive, either by choice or injury, to begin normal cycling *only* with a gain in body weight. However, both Warren (1980) and Abraham et al. (1982) reported that ballet dancers improved menstrual status during vacations or periods of enforced rest without appreciable change in body weight. Both investigators concluded that strenuous exercise, rather than body weight or composition, was the important factor in determining menstrual regularity.

One difficulty in delineating the role of body composition in athletic amenorrhea is that thin runners also tend to be the better runners. These women train more intensely, run faster, and are more competitive, confounding the effect of low body fat with a high physical and psychic energy drain. To further confuse the issue Lutter & Cushman (1982) reported that of 14 women in their survey who had low body weight and high mileage, 50% were oligo/amenorrheic; the other 50% had regular cycles. Obviously the relationship between body composition and menstrual irregularity is less than perfect.

The hypothesized mechanism by which body fat might affect the menstrual cycle is related to the role of fat cells in the aromatization of androgens to estrone. According to Frisch et al. (1981), adipose tissue is an important extragonadal source of estrogen. They suggest that the loss of this source in lean athletes may alter the feedback mechanisms in the hypothalamic-pituitary-ovarian axis. To date no one has examined the gonadotropin and steroid patterns before and after weight changes with accompanying changes in menstrual function. A report by Fishman (1980) that peripheral aromatization of androgens to estrone does not decrease when obese women lose weight indicates the complexity of the relationship. Presently it appears that neither low body fat or a marked decrease in body weight entirely explains the incidence of oligo/amenorrhea in female athletes. It is more likely that body composition interacts with other factors involved in strenuous exercise or with individual characteristics of some women athletes.

Investigation into the neuroendocrine response to exercise as it relates to the menstrual cycle is still in a development stage. Numerous problems relating to protocol, technique, adherence, and expense make it very difficult to undertake these studies in the comprehensive manner required to test the hypothesis that hormonal changes with exercise are responsible for athletic oligo/amenorrhea. Generally the studies can be divided into two categories: evaluating the chronic effects of exercise by measuring basal levels of hormones, or studying acute effects by determining differences in hormone levels before and after exercise. A basic problem is interpreting the concentration levels once they are determined. For example, an increase in serum estradiol may represent increased secretion, decreased clearance, or failure to account for hemoconcentration following exercise. Keizer, Kuipers, Verstapper, and Janssen (1982) are quite emphatic in asserting that concentration per se does not reflect biological activity and ignores the changes in steroid binding dynamics resulting from increase in blood temperature and competition between testosterone and estradiol for binding sites. However, present attempts to relate exercise-induced changes in gonadotropins and steroids to menstrual regularity rely on concentrations.

The chronic effects of exercise on the hormonal patterns of oligo/amenorrheic athletes have been inferred from single samples of plasma or serum obtained at intervals which vary from study to study. To date, there are no published reports of patterns established by daily sampling of blood from amenorrheic athletes throughout a time period equivalent to a normal cycle (26-30 days). Dale et al. (1979) drew weekly samples from runners, joggers, and nonrunning controls and reported anovulating women in each group, ranging from 17% in the control group to 50% for the runners. Hormone patterns for all anovulating women were noncyclic. Unfortunately, the data were not reported for cyclic and noncyclic women by activity group. Because LH and FSH were consistently low in the anovulatory women, the authors concluded that the source of the problem was in the hypothalamus and/or pituitary area.

The only two studies to use a daily sampling technique involved eumenorrheic rather than amenorrheic athletes, but the results were intriguing (Bonen et al., 1981; Shangold et al., 1979). In both cases, the hormone profiles departed from the norm even though the subjects were cycling regularly. A shortened luteal phase was observed in both studies with low levels of progesterone during the luteal phase. Bonen et al. (1981) conjecture that an imbalance of the gonadotropins during the follicular phase result in an immature corpus luteum which is unable to produce normal amounts of progesterone in the luteal phase. This hypothesis will require further confirmation since Shangold et al. (1979) found no difference in FSH levels between a normal cycle and one with a shortened luteal phase.

It is unfortunate but understandable that there is not more data on the effects of chronic exercise on the hormonal profiles of oligo/amenorrheic athletes across time. Not only are the hormonal analyses expensive, but the investigator must also recruit a large number of women, amenorrheic and eumenorrheic, who are willing to submit to daily venapunctures for 30 days. Nevertheless, this is the only way to identify differences in daily fluctuations of gonadotropins and ovarian hormones between these two groups.

A number of investigators have examined the acute hormonal response to a single exercise bout, but none have included oligo/amenorrheic athletes. Apparently the primary purpose of these investigations was to determine if the response of the gonadotropins and steroids to activity might conceivably affect the functioning of the hypothalamic-pituitary-ovarian axis and lead to menstrual dysfunction. Three of the studies (Bonen et al., 1979; Jurkowski et al., 1978; Shangold et al., 1981) used a similar duration and intensity of exercise, and illustrate the changes in concentration that follow 30-40 minutes of exercise at ~ 70% $\dot{V}O_{2max}$. All three reported a significant increase in progesterone during the luteal phase; Bonen et al. (1979) and Shangold et al. (1981) also noted an increase in the follicular phase. Estradiol was also elevated during the luteal phase in two of the studies (Bonen et al., 1979; Jurkowski et al., 1978), but there was no change in the follicular phase. There were mixed results also with FSH. Only Jurkowski et al. (1978) reported a significant rise in the follicular phase; no one observed a change during the luteal phase. LH was reported as unchanged by exercise in both phases of the cycle in all three studies.

Swimmers, runners, and weight lifters have all increased their testosterone levels following exercise, but the concentrations are still within the normal range for women and well below the values for men (Fahey, Rolph, Moungmee, Nagel, & Mortara, 1976; Shangold et al., 1981; Sutton, Coleman, Casey, & Lazarus, 1973). Because women with hyperprolactinemia are also amenorrheic, some investigators have measured prolactin levels before and after exercise and have found significant increases (Brisson, Volle, DeCarufel, Desharnais, & Tanaka, 1980; Noel, Dimond, Earl, & Frantz, 1972; Shangold et al., 1981).

Whether the increased concentration of gonadal hormones is related to an increase in secretion or a decrease in clearance cannot be determined from these studies. Keizer, Poortman, and Bunnik (1980) have shown a decrease in metabolic clearance rate of estradiol following 10 minutes of exercise at 70% $\dot{V}O_{2max}$, and most of the authors cited above suggest decreased degradation rather than increased production as the explanation for their observations. Nevertheless, the concentration is increased and may remain high for a considerable period of time in endurance athletes who train for an hour or more once or twice a day. Yet to be determined is whether the increase is of physiologic significance; that is, are the concentrations at a level capable of influencing events along the hypothalamic-pituitary-ovarian axis?

Evidence to support the psychological theory of athletic amenorrhea is lacking. Yet this would seem to be a productive area for research because it is a common observation that mental stress, such as a sudden change in lifestyle, a death in the family, or other distressing personal experience, may cause the menses to cease (Prior, 1982). Baker (1981) suggests that the stress associated with competition and arduous training schedules may have a direct effect on the hypothalamus via the neurotransmitters. However, in the only study to employ psychological tests to discriminate between amenorrheic and eumenorrheic runners, no significant differences occurred between groups in any psychological variable (Schwartz et al., 1981). Until researchers can provide more tangible evidence of a link between mental stress and athletic amenorrhea, this theory will remain untested.

The etiology of athletic oligo/amenorrhea may be of interest to the scientist, but the long-term consequences of the condition are the primary concern for the athlete. Her concerns revolve around three main issues: Is the oligo/amenorrhea a benign and reversible condition? Are there any problems associated with the failure of the ovarian hormones to cycle regularly once a month? And will there be any lasting effect on reproductive functions?

Shangold (1982) makes an important point regarding the first question. Amenorrheic athletes should not assume the amenorrhea was induced by exercise. A number of pathological conditions are marked by cessation of menses, and the female athlete is not immune to problems that afflict women in general. Shangold (1982) recommends that oligo/amenorrheic athletes consult their physician if the condition has existed longer than a year, did not coincide with the initiation of strenuous exercise, or if regular cycles do not resume when training ceases. If the oligo/amenorrhea is related solely to activity habits, the prognosis is good. Many studies (Abraham et al., 1982; Erdelyi, 1962; Shangold et al., 1979; Warren, 1980) report a resumption of menses when training intensity decreases or the activity is discontinued.

In regard to the second question, it should be noted that not all oligo/amenorrheic athletes are hypoestrogenic. Some women have normal levels of estrogen but simply fail to ovulate. Since normal luteal levels of progesterone are not present, menses will not occur. In these cases the physician may prescribe progesterone therapy to avoid problems associated with endometrial hyperplasia (Prior, 1982; Shangold, 1982). Although the long-term effects of low estrogen levels are still speculative at the present time, the amenorrheic athlete should be aware of potential problems. A recent report at the Endocrine Society Annual Meeting in 1982 received wide media attention when the investigators suggested that amenorrheic athletes are at risk for developing osteoporosis (Gonzales, 1982), a condition associated with decreased estrogen production in postmenopausal women. Obviously this study must be replicated before the concept of premature osteoporosis in young amenorrheic athletes is accepted as fact. Among other possible effects of estrogen deficiency are vaginal atrophy, hypertension, and cardiovascular problems (Prior, 1982; Shangold, 1982), none of which have been documented.

The evidence regarding reproductive function is largely anecdotal and retrospective. It is encouraging to hear about former amenorrheic athletes giving birth to normal healthy children, but there is no data to document the circumstances surrounding these events. Most investigators in the field emphasize the need for controlled prospective studies to explore all the effects of the hormonal changes that occur during the strenuous training of women athletes. In the meantime no one is suggesting that women make any change in their active lifestyle. The beneficial effects of vigorous activity are well documented and women should share in these benefits while the investigation into exercise-associated amenorrhea continues.

REFERENCES

ABRAHAM, S.F., Beumont, P.J.V., Fraser, I.S., & Llewellyn-Jones, D. Body weight, exercise, and menstrual status among ballet dancers in training. *British Journal of Obstetrics and Gynaecology*, 1982, **89**, 507-510.

ÅSTRAND, P.-O., Eriksson, B.O., Nylander, I., Engstrom, L., Karlberg, P., Saltin, B., & Thoren, C. Girl swimmers with special reference to respiratory and circulatory adaptation and gynaecological and psychiatric aspects. *Acta Paediatrica*, 1963, **147** (Suppl.), 1-73.

BAKER, E.R. Menstrual dysfunction and hormonal status in athletic women: A review. *Fertility and Sterility*, 1981, **36**, 691-696.

BAKER, E.R., Mathur, R.S., Kirk, R.F., & Williamson, H.O. Female runners and secondary amenorrhea: Correlation with age, parity, mileage and plasma hormonal and sex-hormone-binding globulin concentrations. *Fertility and Sterility*, 1981, **36**, 183-187.

BONEN, A., Belcastro, A.N., Ling, W.Y., & Simpson, A.A. Profiles of selected hormones during menstrual cycles of teenage athletes. *Journal of Applied Physiology: Respiratory, Environmental, and Exercise Physiology*, 1981, **50**, 545-551.

BONEN, A., Ling, W.Y., MacIntyre, K.P., Neil, R., McGrail, J.C., & Belcastro, A.N. Effects of exercise on the serum concentrations of FSH, LH, progesterone, and estradiol. *European Journal of Applied Physiology*, 1979, **42**, 15-23.

BOYDEN, T.W., Pamenter, R.W., Grosso, D., Stanforth, P., Rotkis, T., & Wilmore, J.H. Prolactin responses, menstrual cycles, and body composition of women runners. *Journal of Clinical Endocrinology and Metabolism*, 1982, **54**, 711-714.

BRISSON, G.R., Volle, M.A., DeCarufel, D., Desharnais, M., & Tanaka, M. Exercise-induced dissociation of the blood prolactin response in young women according to their sports habits. *Hormone and Metabolism Research*, 1980, **12**, 201-205.

BULLEN, B.A., Skinner, G.S., McArthur, J.W., & Carr, D.B. Exercise effect upon plasma melatonin levels in women: Possible physiological significance. *Canadian Journal of Applied Sport Science*, 1982, **7**, 90-97.

CARLBERG, K.A., & Riedesel, M.L. Athletic training and body composition as factors in secondary amenorrhea. *Physiologist*, 1979, **22**, 17. (Abstract)

COHEN, J.L., Kim, C.S., May, P.B., & Ertel, N.H. Exercise, body weight, and amenorrhea in professional ballet dancers. *The Physician and Sportsmedicine*, 1982, **10**(4), 92-101.

DALE, E., Gerlach, D.H., & Wilhite, A.L. Menstrual dysfunction in distance runners. *Obstetrics and Gynecology*, 1979, **54**, 47-53.

ERDELYI, G.L. Gynecological survey of female athletes. *Journal of Sports Medicine and Physical Fitness*, 1962, **2**, 174-179.

ERDELYI, G.J. Effect of exercise on the menstrual cycle. *The Physician and Sportsmedicine*, 1976, **4**, 79-81.

FAHEY, T.D., Rolph, R., Moungmee, P., Nagel, J., & Mortara, S. Serum testosterone, body composition, and strength of young adults. *Medicine and Science in Sports*, 1976, **8**, 31-34.

FEICHT, C.B., Johnson, T.S., Martin, B.J., Sparkes, K.E., & Wagner, W.W., Jr. Secondary amenorrhea in athletes. *Lancet*, 1978, **2**, 1145-1146.

FISHMAN, J. Fatness, puberty, and ovulation. *New England Journal of Medicine*, 1980, **303**, 42-43.

FRISCH, R.E. A method of prediction of age of menarche from height and weight at ages 9 through 13 years. *Pediatrics*, 1974, **53**, 384-390.

FRISCH, R.E., Gotz-Welbergen, A.V., McArthur, J.W., Albright, T., Witsch, J., Bullen, B., Birnholz, J., Reed, R.B., & Herman, H. Delayed menarche and amenorrhea of college athletes in relation to age of onset of training. *Journal of the American Medical Association*, 1981, **246**, 1559-1563.

FRISCH, R.E., & McArthur, J.W. Menstrual cycles: Fatness as a determinant of minimum weight for height necessary for the maintenance or onset. *Science*, 1974, **185**, 949-951.

FRISCH, R.E., & Revelle, R. Height and weight at menarche and a hypothesis of critical body weights and adolescent events. *Science*, 1970, **169**, 397-398.

FRISCH, R.E., Revelle, R., & Cook, S. Components of weight at menarche and the initiation of the adolescent growth spurt in girls: Estimated total water, lean body weight, and fat. *Human Biology*, 1974, **45**, 469.

FRISCH, R.E., Wyshak, G., & Vincent, L. Delayed menarche and amenorrhea in ballet dancers. *New England Journal of Medicine*, 1980, **303**, 17-19.

GONZALES, E.R. Premature bone loss found in some nonmenstruating sportswomen. *Journal of the American Medical Association*, 1982, **248**, 513-514.

JACOBS, H.S. Amenorrhea in athletes. *British Journal of Obstetrics and Gynaecology*, 1982, **89**, 498-499.

JURKOWSKI, J.E., Jones, N.L., Walker, W.C., Younglai, E.V., & Sutton, J.R. Ovarian hormonal responses to exercise. *Journal of Applied Physiology: Respiratory, Environmental, and Exercise Physiology*, 1978, **44**, 109-114.

KEIZER, H.A., Kuipers, H., Verstapper, F.T.J., & Janssen, E. Limitations of concentration measurement for evaluation of endocrine status of exercising women. *Canadian Journal of Applied Sport Science*, 1982, **7**, 79-84.

KEIZER, H.A., Poortman, J., & Bunnik, G.S.J. Influence of physical exercise on sex hormone metabolism. *Journal of Applied Physiology: Respiratory, Environmental, and Exercise Physiology*, 1980, **48**, 765-769.

KNOBIL, E. The neuroendocrine control of the menstrual cycle. *Recent Progress in Hormone Research*, 1980, **36**, 53-87.

LUTTER, J.M., & Cushman, S. Menstrual patterns in female runners. *Physician and Sportsmedicine*, 1982, **10**(9), 60-72.

NOEL, G.L., Dimond, R.C., Earl, J.M., & Frantz, A.G. Human prolactin and growth hormone release during surgery and other conditions of stress. *Journal of Clinical Endocrinology and Metabolism*, 1972, **35**, 840-851.

PRIOR, J.C. Endocrine 'conditioning' with endurance training: A preliminary review. *Canadian Journal of Applied Sport Science*, 1982, **7**, 148-157.

REBAR, R.W., & Cumming, D.C. Reproductive function in women athletes. *Journal of the American Medical Association*, 1981, **246**, 1590.

REEVES, J. Estimating fatness. *Science*, 1979, **204**, 881.

SANBORN, C.F., Martin, B.J., & Wagner, W.W., Jr. Is athletic amenorrhea specific to runners? *American Journal of Obstetrics and Gynecology*, 1982, **143**, 859-861.

SCHWARTZ, B., Cumming, D., Riordan, E., Selye, M., Yen, S., & Rebar, R. Exercise-associated amenorrhea: A distinct entity? *American Journal of Obstetrics and Gynecology*, 1981, **141**, 662-670.

SHANGOLD, M. Menstrual irregularity in athletes: Basic principles, evaluation, and treatment. *Canadian Journal of Applied Sport Science*, 1982, **7**, 68-73.

SHANGOLD, M., Freeman, R., Thysen, B., & Gatz, M. The relationship between long-distance running, plasma progesterone, and luteal phase length. *Fertility and Sterility*, 1979, **31**, 130-133.

SHANGOLD, M.M., Gatz, M.L., & Thysen, B. Acute effects of exercise on plasma concentrations of prolactin and testosterone in recreational women runners. *Fertility and Sterility*, 1981, **35**, 699-702.

SHANGOLD, M.M., & Levine, H.S. The effect of marathon training upon menstrual function. *American Journal of Obstetrics and Gynecology*, 1982, **143**, 862-869.

SPEROFF, L., & Redwine, D.B. Exercise and menstrual function. *The Physician and Sportsmedicine*, 1980, **8**(5), 41-52.

SUTTON, J.R., Coleman, M.J., Casey, J., & Lazarus, L. Androgen responses during physical exercise. *British Medical Journal*, 1973, **1**, 520-522.

TRUSSELL, J. Menarche and fatness: Reexamination of the critical body composition hypothesis. *Science*, 1978, **200**, 1506-1509.

TURGEON, J.L. Neural control of ovulation. *Physiologist*, 1980, **23**(3), 56-62.

WAKAT, D.K., Sweeney, K.A., & Rogol, A.D. Reproductive system function in women cross-country runners. *Medicine and Science in Sports and Exercise*, 1982, **14**, 263-269.

WARREN, M.P. The effects of exercise on pubertal progression and reproductive function in girls. *Journal of Clinical Endocrinology and Metabolism*, 1980, **51**, 1150-1157.

WEBB, J.L., Millan, D.L., & Stottz, C.J. Gynecological survey of American female athletes competing at the Montreal Olympic Games. *Journal of Sport Medicine and Physical Fitness*, 1979, **19**, 405-412.

WILMORE, J.H., Brown, C.H., & Davis, J.A. Body physique and composition of the female distance runner. *Annals of the New York Academy of Science*, 1977, **301**, 764-776.

Physical Activity and Mental Health

William P. Morgan
University of Wisconsin-Madison

To affect the quality of the day, that is the highest of arts.
— Henry David Thoreau

There has been a tendency for exercise and sport scientists to focus their attention on physical health and the ways in which physical activity might enhance longevity. An equally important consideration is the extent to which physical activity influences mental health and the associated "quality" of one's life. In other words, involvement in regular, vigorous physical activity may or may not increase the number of years lived, but it may well enhance the quality of years lived. Support for this view comes from several sources. The basic premise is that positive mental health enhances the quality of life, and the basic question is whether or not physical activity can help develop or maintain mental health. Support for this view will be considered here.

Psychiatrists have long maintained that physical well-being is associated with positive mental health. The physiological benefits of physical activity are well documented, and convincing evidence on this topic is presented elsewhere in this book. It is also believed that acute physical activity helps in venting tensions, which in turn leads to sustained mental health across time. This concept implies that both *acute* and *chronic* psychologic effects are associated with physical activity; that is, the chronic or long-term effect is thought to occur via the venting of tensions at an acute level. Another view expressed by mental health workers is that regular exercise not only reduces anxiety, but it also develops higher tolerance levels. This commonly held view implies that physically fit individuals are better able to cope with stress than are sedentary individuals. These traditional ideas are based on the monistic concept of mind-body unity, and although ample philosophical and theoretical support for such a view exists, there has not been much empirical evidence deal-

Preparation of this article was supported in part by National Heart, Lung and Blood Institute Grant HL 25786.

ing with psychologic beneficience of physical activity, at least not at a causal level. Also, the evidential issue can be likened to August Derleth's entry in his *Countryman's Journal* (1963), in which he stated,

> Grandfather Derleth having died in his ninetieth year, his grave was being dug today, while a soft rain fell. It troubled mother, who said, 'Rain in an open grave, another death within a year.' She did not remember where she had learned this superstition. When asked for the source or evidence she replied, 'I always heard it. Mama said it—why it's generally believed.' (p. 188)

In many ways the traditional views outlined above are similar; that is, it is generally believed that exercise is good for your emotional health. The limited evidence supporting this belief will be explored here.

There is a subtle danger in describing the psychologic *or* physiologic effects of exercise because adaptations are seldom, if ever, limited to psychic or somatic change alone. It is only our vantage point that permits us to talk of an event as being psychological or physiological in nature. Although exercise physiologists seem to believe the body does not have a head, and sport psychologists operate as though the head does not have a body, it is obvious to any casual observer that involvement in exercise and sport represents a rather complex psychobiologic process. It is only convenience and caprice that enable the psychologist and physiologist to operate at other than a monistic level.

Philosophers, sages, mystics, and transcendentalists have historically agreed on the unity of mind and body. Henry David Thoreau, for example, made the following comment in his *Journal* on June 21, 1840:

> I never feel that I am inspired unless my body is also. They are fatally mistaken who think while they strive with their minds that they may suffer their bodies to stagnate in luxury and sloth. The body is the first proselyte the soul makes. The whole duty of man may be expressed in one line . . . make to yourself a perfect body. (p. 42)

A more recent introspective statement about the psychic effects of exercise comes from Arnold J. Mandell's introduction to "The *Second* Second Wind" (1979), in which he quotes from his own volume entitled *Coming of Middle Age: A Journey*. The analysis reads in part,

> Thirty minutes out, and something lifts. Legs and arms become light and rhythmic. The fatigue goes away and feelings of power begin. I think I'll run twenty-five miles today. I'll double the size of the research grant request. I'll have that talk with the dean . . . Then, sometime into the second hour comes the spooky time. Colors are bright and beautiful, water sparkles, clouds breathe, and my body, swimming, detaches from the earth. A loving contentment invades the basement of my mind, and

thoughts bubble up without trails. I find the place I need to live if I'm going to live. A cosmic view and peace are located between six and ten miles of running. (p. 37)

Individuals experience many different sensations during and following exercise and sport activities. The introspective account presented above illustrates one individual's description of the running experience. Much, perhaps most, of the literature dealing with the psychologic effects of exercise has relied on the use of objective self-report inventories designed to measure constructs such as anxiety and depression. These questionnaires usually contain a yes-no, true-false, or Likert format. The extent to which these inventories can tap the psychometric domain of significance to the exerciser has not been evaluated. In other words, an investigator may employ an objective, reliable, valid test of anxiety or depression to quantify the psychologic effects of exercise, only to find that no "effects" have taken place when, in fact, there may have been numerous effects (e.g., aggression, hostility, strength, power, fear, peace, sleep patterns, and so on). Sport psychologists have debated for years about the "best" or "appropriate" psychological test to employ. The answer is actually rather simple. The measure to be employed in a particular investigation should be based upon the question being asked!

In addition to the traditional and philosophical views concerning the psychologic benefits of exercise, there is also a related argument based upon anthropological views. Lee and DeVore (1968) have pointed out, for example, that we have been hunter-gatherers for 99% of our history. And Lewin (1981) has noted that hunting and gathering not only dominated much of human history, but it was a way of life that "provided a surprising degree of security and leisure" (p. 41).

Cohen (1981) has stated, "It is a striking fact that largely irreversible sedentism emerges in a remarkably parallel manner in various parts of the world over the past 15,000 years" (p. 41). It remains a puzzle why a universal shift to agriculture took place over a relatively short period of time. In this context, Lee and DeVore (1968) have pointed out that:

> Interplanetary archeologists of the future will classify our planet as one in which a very long and stable period of small-scale hunting and gathering was followed by an apparently instantaneous efflorescence of technology and society leading rapidly to extinction. 'Stratigraphically,' the origin of agriculture and thermonuclear destruction will appear as essentially simultaneous. (p. 3)

While there is some question as to how well the modern day inhabitant of the planet earth has adapted to the stress that characterizes 20th century society, anthropological and archeological evidence seems to support the view that we are hunter-gatherers — at least in evolutionary and historical terms. The psychobiological cost of masquerading as perfumed men and women in three-piece suits remains to be demonstrated! At any rate, a case can be made for exercise on the grounds that it will help us to become that which we were meant to be — hunter-gatherers (Bettinger & Baumhoff, 1982; Cohen, 1981; Lee & DeVore, 1968; Lewin, 1981).

There is also comparative evidence that vigorous physical activity has a psychologic impact. Weber and Lee (1968), for example, randomly assigned 48 male albino rats to: a) a sedentary condition which restricted them to a standard 10 × 8 × 7-inch cage; b) a voluntary exercise condition in which they were housed in a similar cage but were allowed access to a revolving exercise wheel; and c) forced exercise consisting of daily swims with an overload of 2% of the animal's body weight attached. The experimental period ranged from the animal's 31st day of life to the 65th day of life. The animals were then evaluated on a standard test of "emotionality" consisting of the open-field test. The sedentary and voluntary exercise groups did not differ on any comparison, but the forced exercise group was observed to be less emotional than the sedentary and voluntary exercise groups on all comparisons. These results indicate that prepuberty exercise influences emotionality and response to a stressor introduced during puberty.

The work of Weber and Lee (1968) is cited primarily to illustrate the point that research on animals suggests that vigorous exercise has a positive influence on psychological measures involving various animal models. The reasons for this adaptation are not entirely clear, but theoretical (Morgan, Olson, & Pedersen, 1982) and empirical evidence (Olson & Morgan, 1982) suggests that brain neurotransmitter levels are implicated.

Research involving humans is consistent with the animal literature. For example, there is evidence of an inverse relationship between physical fitness and psychopathology; that is, the higher the level of physical fitness, the lower the degree of psychopathology. This literature is based almost entirely on hospitalized psychiatric patients, and physical fitness has usually been operationalized in a unidimensional or single variable context. Typical studies have employed measures of muscular strength, muscular endurance, agility, physical work capacity, *or* aerobic power, but few attempts to quantify physical fitness in a multidimensional manner have been carried out. Several reviews of this literature have appeared over the past decade (Folkins & Sime, 1981; Morgan, 1969, 1974, 1977b, 1981, 1982). Most of the research presented in these reviews has been cross-sectional, and psychological differences between physically active and sedentary groups have usually been attributed to the different exercise patterns of such groups. Another approach has involved the psychological comparison of groups of individuals differing in levels of physical fitness, and any observed psychological differences were thought to result from exercise.

Common interpretations of this correlational research are questionable for at least three reasons. First, Klissouras (1970) has reported that maximal aerobic power, one of the best measures of overall physical fitness, has a large heritability component. Second, there is evidence that personality structure remains quite stable across the life span (Kelly, 1955; Leon, Gillum, Gillum, & Gouze, 1979; Morgan, Montoye, Brown, & Johnson, Note 1). In the recent report by Morgan et al. (Note 1), for example, it was possible to predict mood state in 38-year-old males from personality data collected at age 18, and the accuracy of this prediction ranged from 70 to 75%. Third, there is evidence that individuals who become involved in sports and exercise may already differ psychologically, as well as physiologically, from those who are sedentary (Morgan, 1982). Therefore, while it is true that elite female and male athletes differ significantly from the general population on variables such as anxiety, depression, vigor, fatigue, and confusion (i.e., "iceberg" profile), there is a lack of evidence to support the view that exercise and sport has *caused* these differences (Johnson & Morgan, 1981; Morgan, 1980).

The view that physical fitness training leads to improved mental health (Folkins & Sime, 1981) should be considered as hypothetical rather than factual. The correlational, cross-sectional, and epidemiological data upon which this hypothesis is based reflects *necessary* rather than *sufficient* evidence. Demonstration of *causality*, as opposed to mere *association*, is unlikely to occur unless well-designed intervention studies are carried out. The literature in this field reveals that much of the intervention research is based upon quasi-experimental designs in which subjects are seldom assigned to treatments in a random manner, control groups have seldom been utilized, placebo groups have been extremely rare, and investigators have typically attributed observed psychologic change to the treatment (i.e., exercise). While exercise may have caused the observed changes, there are many alternative hypotheses.

In one of our earliest attempts to evalute the influence of exercise on depression, groups of middle-aged men participated in various training programs (e.g., jogging, swimming, circuit training, and cycling). The results were compared with controls who remained sedentary throughout the 6-week training program (Morgan, Roberts, Brand, & Feinerman, 1970). The exercise groups became more physically fit whereas the control group did not, but none of the groups had changes in depression. Eleven of the subjects who exercised manifested depression of clinical significance at the outset of the study, and each of these individuals experienced a decrease in depression with training. The mean decrease was statistically significant for this group of moderately depressed subjects, and the improvement was independent of the type of exercise pursued. This study, and others as well, suggests that individuals scoring within the normal range on a depression scale are not likely to become "more normal" with chronic exercise training. Also, it would be inappropriate to suggest that exercise training was responsible for the reduction in depression observed in this study. The observed effect may have been due to statistical regression, the special attention or "Hawthorne" effect, diversion from stress, alteration of health habits and patterns (e.g., alcohol, tobacco and drug use, sleep patterns, etc.), and/or exercise. Of course, exercise enthusiasts tend to use such evidence in support of exercise, but such views are purely speculative.

Most of the intervention studies carried out so far have been characterized by serious flaws in experimental design. A possible exception to this is the exploratory work of Greist, Klein, Eischens, Faris, Gurman, & Morgan (1979), which demonstrated that aerobic exercise performed for 12 weeks not only was associated with a reduction in depression, but the improvement was superior to one form of traditional psychotherapy and equal to a second in its anti-depressant action.

The research of Greist et al. (1979) is important for several reasons. First, rather than comparing exercise with "nothing" (i.e., a control group), a comparison was made with traditional forms of psychotherapy. Second, considering the expense associated with psychotherapy, running therapy is less expensive. Third, all but one of the patients in the running group were free of depressive symptoms at 12 months of follow-up, whereas half of the psychotherapy patients had returned for treatment. Fourth, the subjects in this investigation were outpatients suffering from moderate or mild depression, and such patients often do not respond well to antidepressant medication. Indeed, medication often worsens their condition even though the same medication usually improves the condition of the severely depressed. Therefore, exercise may offer a nonpharmacologic alternative in treating mild depression. It has also been reported that acute physical activity is comparable to a commonly prescribed tranquilizer, meprobamate, in reducing tension (deVries & Adams, 1972).

The failure to demonstrate psychological changes from exercise intervention may reflect the nature of the measure(s) employed. It is possible, for example, that significant and important changes have taken place, but these alterations were not apparent because the appropriate construct was not studied. Measures of anxiety and depression sometimes do not change following aerobic fitness programs even though substantial alterations in aerobic power occur. This finding is often perplexing because most subjects frequently report that they now "feel better." Sonstroem (1974, 1976, 1981) has developed a psychobiologic model that lends itself to application in this area. The model posits that physical activity leads to improved physical fitness, and there is substantial support for this view. The model further specifies that improved physical fitness results in an increased estimation of physical ability, which in turn is thought to enhance self-esteem. Increases in estimation of physical ability are thought to lead to increased attraction to physical activity, followed by further increases in physical fitness, estimation of physical ability, and self-esteem. Sonstroem (1976) has validated a self-report scale for use in quantifying physical estimation and attraction to physical activity, and the scale has been adapted for use with adults (Morgan, 1977a).

The efficacy of Sontroem's model was evaluated by Morgan and Pollock (Note 2), who administered the Physical Estimation and Attraction Scale (PEAS) to 60 men prior to beginning a fitness program. Ten subjects served as controls and the remaining 50 subjects took part in one of several training programs. After 10 weeks of training, the PEAS was administered again to the exercise groups and the control group; it was also administered at the conclusion of the study. The results of this investigation are summarized in Figure 1. Each of the exercise groups had mean increases in estimation of physical ability ranging from 3.5 to 5.2 raw score units on the PEAS. The mean increase for the five exercise groups was 4.5, and the control group did not change. The data were analyzed by means of a repeated measures ANOVA for multifactor experiments, and the analysis yielded F ratios of 0.67 ($P > .05$) for groups, 27.67 ($P < .01$) for trials, and 1.27 ($P > .05$) for the groups by trials interaction. A further probe with the Newman-Keuls procedure revealed

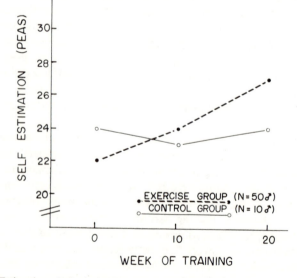

Figure 1. Estimation of physical ability before, during, and following a 20-week exercise program.

that the exercise group scored significantly higher on self-estimation at Trial 3 in comparison to Trial 1. The evaluation at Trial 2 (10th week) did not differ from Trial 1 or Trial 3 for the exercise group, and the control group did not experience changes at any point.

These findings are of interest from several standpoints. First, self-estimation was found to improve significantly in those subjects who exercised. Second, the improvement was not apparent following 10 weeks of training. This is quite important because it is well documented that most individuals who drop out of an exercise program do so prior to the 10th week (Morgan, 1977a). Also, Greist et al. (1979) found that the exercise effects noted for depressed outpatients did not occur until later in the training program. This is important because most individuals who discontinue formal exercise programs do so prior to the time that psychological gains have been found to occur.

Research involving longitudinal intervention paradigms has not yielded results as consistent as those observed in correlational and epidemiological studies. Also, athletes have consistently been found to possess more desirable mental health profiles than nonathletes (Johnson & Morgan, 1981; Morgan, 1972, 1976, 1980; Morgan & Pollock, 1977), but these differences have not been clinically significant. It is also quite possible that such differences exist from the outset rather than being due to involvement in sports. Correlational research involving hospitalized psychiatric patients has also indirectly supported the view that exercise and mental health are linked. Correlational evidence alone, with patients or normals, is not a *sufficient* form of evidence. However, it does represent *necessary* evidence and is consonant with theoretical expectations. This issue will not be resolved until well-designed intervention trials are conducted. Most investigations in this area have historically compared exercise with nothing (i.e., control), and investigators have assumed that observed changes were due to the exercise. An exception to this is the work of Greist et al. (1979), who reported that running therapy is equal to one form of psychotherapy and superior to a second in treating moderate depression.

It is possible that chronic or long-term effects do not occur for most individuals, but it is also possible that these same individuals experience acute psychologic effects on a daily basis. The limited research involving the psychological effects of acute physical activity has been concerned with anxiety. deVries and associates (deVries, 1968; deVries & Adams, 1972; deVries, Burke, Hopper, & Sloan, 1977) have demonstrated that vigorous physical activity reduces tension as measured electromyographically. This work is summarized in detail by deVries elsewhere in this book. A series of studies from our laboratory has demonstrated that vigorous physical activity (i.e., 70-80% of maximal aerobic power) is associated with a significant decrease in state anxiety (Morgan,

1979) as measured by the state form of Spielberger's State-Trait Anxiety Scale (Spielberger, Gorsuch, & Luschene, 1970). The intensity of the exercise in these studies was sufficient to provoke significant elevations in plasma epinephrine and norepinephrine (Morgan, Horstman, Cymerman, & Stokes, 1983). In related research, exercise of light to moderate intensities was not found to decrease anxiety (Morgan, Roberts, & Feinerman, 1971; Sime, 1977).

It is not clear why state anxiety decreases following vigorous, acute physical activity. Exercise enthusiasts are quick to propose that the physical activity reduces the tension, but there is little support for such a view. Also, there is evidence that the decreased anxiety observed following exercise may be the result of "distraction," or what Bahrke & Morgan have termed "time out" therapy. In the study by Bahrke & Morgan (1978), 75 men were randomly assigned to an exercise, meditation, or placebo (quiet rest) condition. The subjects were evaluated on state anxiety before the treatments and again at 1 and 10 minutes post-exercise. The exercise consisted of walking on a motor-driven treadmill for 20 minutes at 70% of maximal aerobic power; the meditation consisted of practicing Benson's Relaxation Response for 20 minutes in a sound-filtered room; and the placebo condition consisted of resting quietly in the same sound-filtered room while oxygen consumption, heart rate, and skin temperature were monitored. In other words, the placebo group received special attention but they were not instructed in the relaxation response. The results of this experiment are presented in Figure 2.

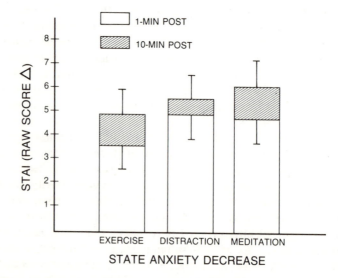

Figure 2. Decreases in state anxiety 1 and 10 minutes following experimental manipulations consisting of exercise (N = 25), distraction (N = 25), and non-cultic meditation (N = 25).

It was predicted that both exercise and meditation would lead to significant decreases in state anxiety, and this hypothesis was confirmed. The magnitude of the decrease did not differ in the two groups, and most of the change was observed within 1 minute following the cessation of exercise. The decrease in state anxiety observed for the "distraction" or placebo group was not expected, and the magnitude of the decrease for this group did not differ from that observed for the exercise or meditation groups. This serendipitous finding may mean that merely resting quietly in a sound-filtered room has the same antianxiety effect as does exercise and meditation. In a somewhat related investigation, Michaels, Huber, and McCann (1976) observed that quiet rest was just as effective as transcendental meditation in reducing plasma levels of epinephrine, norepinephrine, and lactate. The biochemical work of Michaels et al. (1976) can be used to explain the reduced anxiety in the "distraction" group studied by Bahrke and Morgan (1978), since lactate and catecholamine metabolism have both been implicated in anxiety states.

Recent work at the University of Pennsylvania has shown that resting quietly in a comfortable chair while watching fish swimming in an aquarium will reduce blood pressure in the observer. Earlier work by Katcher and Friedmann (1980) supports the potential health value of owning a pet, and these investigators maintain that the physical and emotional benefits of owning a pet extend beyond exercise-mediated effects (e.g., walking one's dog). In other words, paying attention to a pet may have the effect of distracting an individual from stress in his or her environment.

It is possible that the immediate antianxiety effect of exercise and "time out" therapy (i.e., doing nothing) is essentially the same, but the time course or dose-response curve for the two treatments may differ. This possibility has yet to be evaluated, but Seemann (1978) has reported on the time course of anxiety changes following exercise. Men and women were evaluated before and after aerobic exercise that lasted approximately 45 minutes. Both groups experienced significant decreases in state anxiety as previously reported by others. Seemann (1978) evaluated these subjects across the following 24-hour period and found that both groups returned to the pre-exercise level within 4 to 6 hours; and the mean state anxiety levels at 24 hours post-exercise were identical to the values observed prior to the exercise session. This research suggests that a major benefit of regular exercise might be its ability to reduce anxiety on a daily basis and prevent the onset of chronic anxiety.

Seemann's work may also explain why some investigators have failed to observe changes in anxiety across time even though the subjects report that they feel better. In other words, the major psychological benefit would be the transient or acute tension reduction following each exercise bout. This research does not, however, address the question of whether or not the persistence of exercise effects for 4-6 hours differs from the time course associated with meditation or simple rest breaks. This particular question is being studied by Raglin (Note 3) and should be clarified soon.

The "distraction" hypothesis advanced by Bahrke and Morgan (1978) addresses the issue of whether or not exercise *per se* is the crucial variable in producing the observed decreases in state anxiety. Their work does not support or rule out such a possibility, but it does suggest that comparable antianxiety effects can be produced with simple rest breaks. Thoreau (1841) wrote in his *Journal* on April 26, 1841 that "It is a great art to saunter" (p. 75). In his section on "Walking," which appeared in *Excursions*, he stated,

> I think that I cannot preserve my health and spirits, unless I spend four hours a day at least—and it is commonly more than that—sauntering through the woods and over the hills and fields, absolutely free from all worldly engagements. (p. 75)

Did sauntering *per se* preserve Thoreau's health and spirits, or did distraction from his "worldly engagements" bring about the preservation? Of course, we do not know. It is quite apparent that vigorous physical activity brings about physiological changes that would not be expected with mere distraction in the form of meditation or "time out" from one's regular activities. Increases in heart rate, oxygen consumption, ventilatory minute volume, core temperature, and plasma catecholamine levels occur with exercise, whereas the reverse would be expected with relaxation strategies. It is possible, of course, that central psychobiochemical alterations take place with both exercise and relaxation. This possibility is tenable but it has not been evaluated systematically.

Beta-endorphin and beta-lipotropin activity may be implicated in exercise-induced euphoric states, but there is a lack of agreement on this view (Morgan, 1982). However, theoretical, correlational, retrospective epidemiological, and experimental evidence suggests that vigorous physical activity, both acute and chronic, is *associated* with improved *affective states*. This finding is especially true for individuals who are moderately depressed or anxious. The major challenge now concerns "why" exercise is associated with improved affect; current attempts to elucidate the mechanisms underlying such change may ultimately provide a plausible explanation. In the meantime, may I suggest that we continue our exercise programs on the basis of Thoreau's advice in *Walden* ("Higher Laws"): "Every man is the builder of a temple called his body . . . We are all sculptors and painters, and our material is our own flesh and blood and bones" (p. 109).

REFERENCE NOTES

1. Morgan, W.P., Montoye, H.J., Brown, D.R., & Johnson, R.W. *Efficacy of the MMPI in predicting health status, health behavior, and quality of life: A 20-year prospective study.* Paper presented at the 18th Annual Symposium on Recent Developments in the Use of the MMPI, Minneapolis, April 1983.
2. Morgan, W.P., & Pollock, M.L. *Influence of chronic physical activity on selected psychological states and traits of police officers* (Technical Report). Rockville, MD: International Association of Chiefs of Police, December 1976.
3. Raglin, J.S. *Influence of acute exercise and "distraction therapy" on state anxiety and blood pressure.* Unpublished manuscript, 1983. (Available from J.S. Raglin, Sport Psychology Laboratory, University of Wisconsin-Madison, 2000 Observatory Drive, Madison, WI 53706.)

REFERENCES

BAHRKE, M.S., & Morgan, W.P. Anxiety reduction following exercise and meditation. *Cognitive Therapy and Research*, 1978, **2**, 323-334.

BETTINGER, R.L., & Baumhoff, M.A. The Numic spread: Great basin cultures in competition. *American Antiquity*, 1982, **47**, 485-503.

COHEN, M. [Disease clue to dawn of agriculture] (R. Lewin, Ed.). *Science*, 1981, **211**, 41.

DERLETH, A. *Countryman's journal.* New York: Meredith, 1963.

deVRIES, H.A. Immediate and long term effects of exercise upon resting muscle action potential. *Journal of Sports Medicine and Physical Fitness*, 1968, **8**, 1-11.

deVRIES, H.A., & Adams, G.M. Electromyographic comparison of single doses of exercise and meprobamate as to effects on muscular relaxation. *American Journal of Physical Medicine*, 1972, **51**, 130-141.

deVRIES, H.A., Burke, R.K., Hopper, R.T., & Sloan, J.H. Efficacy of EMG biofeedback in relaxation training. *American Journal of Physical Medicine*, 1977, **56**, 75-81.

FOLKINS, C.H., & Sime, W.E. Physical fitness training and mental health. *American Psychologist*, 1981, **36**, 373-389.

GREIST, J.H., Klein, M.H., Eischens, R.R., Faris, J., Gurman, A.S., & Morgan, W.P. Running as treatment for depression. *Comprehensive Psychiatry*, 1979, **20**, 41-53.

JOHNSON, R.W., & Morgan, W.P. Personality characteristics of college athletes in different sports. *Scandinavian Journal of Sports Sciences*, 1981, **3**, 41-49.

KATCHER, A.H., & Friedmann, E. Potential health value of pet ownership. *The Compendium on Continuing Education*, 1980, **11**, 117-122.

KELLY, E.L. Consistency of adult personality. *American Psychologist*, 1955, **10**, 659-681.

KLISSOURAS, V. Heritability of adaptive variation. *Journal of Applied Physiology*, 1970, **29**, 358-367.

LEE, R.L., & DeVore, I. (Eds.). *Man the hunter.* Chicago: Aldine, 1968.

LEON, G.R., Gillum, B., Gillum, R., & Gouze, M. Personality stability and change over a 30-year period — Middle age to old age. *Journal of Consulting and Clinical Psychology*, 1979, **47**, 517-524.

LEWIN, R. Disease clue to dawn of agriculture. *Science*, 1981, **211**, 41.

MANDELL, A.J. The *second* second wind. *Psychiatric Annals*, 1979, **9**, 57-68.

MICHAELS, R.R., Huber, M.J., & McCann, D.S. Evaluation of transcendental meditation as a method of reducing stress. *Science*, 1976, **192**, 1242-1244.

MORGAN, W.P. Physical fitness and emotional health: A review. *American Corrective Therapy Journal*, 1969, **23**, 124-127.

MORGAN, W.P. Sport psychology. In R.N. Singer (Ed.), *Psychomotor domain: Movement behavior.* Philadelphia: Lea & Febiger, 1972.

MORGAN, W.P. Exercise and mental disorders. In A.J. Ryan & F.L. Allman (Eds.), *Sports Medicine.* New York: Academic Press, 1974.

MORGAN, W.P. Psychological aspects of sports. In J.C.P. Williams & P.N. Sperryn (Eds.), *Sports medicine.* London: Edward Arnold, 1976.

MORGAN, W.P. Involvement in vigorous physical activity with special reference to adherence. In L.I. Gedvilas & M.E. Kneer (Eds.), *College physical education proceedings.* Chicago: Office of Publications Service, University of Illinois-Chicago Circle, 1977. (a)

MORGAN, W.P. Psychological consequences of vigorous physical activity and sport. In M.G. Scott (Ed.), *The academy papers.* Iowa City, IA: American Academy of Physical Education, 1977. (b)

MORGAN, W.P. Anxiety reduction following acute physical activity. *Psychiatric Annals*, 1979, **9**, 36-45.

MORGAN, W.P. The trait psychology controversy. *Research Quarterly for Exercise and Sport*, 1980, **51**, 50-76.

MORGAN, W.P. Psychological benefits of physical activity. In F.J. Nagle & H.J. Montoye (Eds.), *Exercise, health, and disease.* Springfield, IL: Charles C. Thomas, 1981.

MORGAN, W.P. Psychological effects of exercise. *Behavioral Medicine Update*, 1982, **4**, 25-30.

MORGAN, W.P., Horstman, D.H., Cymerman, A., & Stokes, J. Facilitation of physical performance by means of a cognitive strategy. *Cognitive Therapy and Research*, 1983, **7**, 251-264.

MORGAN, W.P., Olson, E.B., Jr., & Pedersen, N.P. A rat model of psychopathology for use in exercise science. *Medicine and Science in Sports and Exercise*, 1982, **14**, 91-100.

MORGAN, W.P., & Pollock, M.L. Psychologic characterization of the elite distance runner. In P. Milvy (Ed.), *Annals New York Academy of Science*, 1977, **301**, 382-403.

MORGAN, W.P., Roberts, J.A., Brand, F.R., & Feinerman, A.D. Psychological effect of chronic physical activity. *Medicine and Science in Sports*, 1970, **2**, 213-217.

MORGAN, W.P., Roberts, J.A., & Feinerman, A.D. Psychologic effect of acute physical activity. *Archives of Physical Medicine and Rehabilitation*, 1971, **52**, 422-425.

OLSON, E.B., Jr., & Morgan, W.P. Rat brain monoamine levels related to behavioral assessment. *Life Sciences*, 1982, **30**, 2095-2100.

SEEMANN, J.C. *Changes in state anxiety following vigorous exercise.* Unpublished master's thesis, University of Arizona, 1978.

SIME, W.E. A comparison of exercise and meditation in reducing physiological response to stress. *Medicine and Science in Sports*, 1977, **9**, 55.

SONSTROEM, R.J. Attitude testing examining certain psychological correlates of physical activity. *Research Quarterly*, 1974, **45**, 93-103.

SONSTROEM, R.J. The validity of self-perceptions regarding physical and athletic ability. *Medicine and Science in Sports*, 1976, **8**, 126-132.

SONSTROEM, R.J. Exercise and self-esteem: Recommendations for expository research. *Quest*, 1981, **33**, 124-139.

SPIELBERGER, C.D., Gorsuch, R.L., & Lushene, R.E. *Manual for the state-trait anxiety inventory.* Palo Alto: Consulting Psychologists Press, 1970.

THOREAU, H.D. [The natural man: A Thoreau anthology] (R. Epstein & S. Phillips, Eds.). Wheaton, IL: The Theosophical Publishing House, 1978.

WEBER, J.C., & Lee, R.A. Effects of differing prepuberty exercise programs on the emotionality of male albino rats. *Research Quarterly*, 1968, **39**, 748-751.

The Future Agenda

Edward J. Shea
Southern Illinois University

Each president of the Academy, upon departing from office, has a responsibility to thank the members for having had the opportunity to serve and associate with others whose dedication to their work has occupied so prominently a role in their lives. Also, after 2 years of intensively providing direction for the program and other Academy affairs, it is natural to measure the accomplishments during one's presidential tenure against the Academy's stated purposes. And in looking to the future, one also reflects upon the Academy's continuing effectiveness within a constantly changing environment of social, economic, and educational forces that operate upon it.

A review of presidential addresses over the past 15 years reveals these types of expression to be fairly constant. They are reflected in the address titles such as *Let's Take A Stand* (1973), *A New Focus* (1974), *Beyond Research* (1976), *Understanding Relationships* (1977), *A Time For Action* (1978), *Turning The Corner* (1979), *The Academy—Today And Tomorrow* (1980), *The Values That Guide Us* (1981), and *Travelling Hopefully* (1982).

In nearly every instance, presidential addresses pointed to a need to make changes in the organization, in the operating procedures, and in the members' aspirations (Esslinger, 1967); a need to provide direction for the health and growth of the profession (Weiss, 1973); a need to offer a new focus of activities and attention (Jewett, 1974); a need to direct more concerted attention away from the mechanical business procedures and into matters of importance to the Academy and the profession (Alley, 1978); a need to resolve problems that affect the profession and society (Clifton, 1979); a need to transcend subdisciplines that are divisive and to forge bonds of communication, understanding, and a greater loyalty to the broader spectrum of physical education (Barrow, 1980).

I find myself inexorably drawn into the same direction of thought as were preceding presidents. I have, therefore, addressed an agenda for the future of the Academy (with reference, of course, to the immediate past), a future which must contemplate both the changes in the environment that influence the performance of social and academic institutions, and the changing nature of the constituency of such institutions. I shall also advance some proposals for veering from the asymptotic* condition that has long characterized the basic nature of the Academy.

Every educational and social institution must be sensitive to change in the environment that surrounds it and must search its meaning. One of our own, Eleanor Metheny, earlier indicated, "In our time, the pursuit of knowledge in all fields of inquiry has been transformed into a search for the sources of meaning in human life" (Metheny, 1968). Her search dealt with the forms of movement called dance, sport, and exercise.

Louis Alley in his address pointed out, "Any organization that does not change to accommodate to the environment or circumstances in which it finds itself, is doomed for extinction. The Academy is no exception" (Alley, 1978, p. 7).

Change is often a measure of growth. As part of a generation of growth, we have been at the forefront of two major revolutions of the past 20 years. During the social revolution of the 60s and 70s, most rituals of personal interaction and institutional life were radically altered. These changes have affected the way we perceive the future and chart its course. Now, in the 80s, we are in a period of major technological change and the advances being made will have an enormous impact on life in the future. We are witnessing a marriage of Social Thinking (60s, 70s) and Technology (80s).

As a prestigious institution with a responsibility to lead, and therefore to be visible within and outside the profession, the Academy must be a member of the wedding. It must anticipate the effects of the new developments upon the lives of those it serves; it must influence the present ferment; and it must take the lead in providing direction through the remainder of America's third century. The Academy must explore the cutting edge of thought, behavior, and style of those in the forefront of changes related to the art and science of human movement and physical activity. It should delineate the distinctive values it can transmit to an America and a world whose thinking, views, and practices will be affected by the new technology on our professional lives, our leisure time, our educational systems, and the thinking and practices of our children and grandchildren. Home computers and video games are only the tip of the iceberg.

---

*A mathematical term that describes a concept whereby a straight line approaches but never touches a curve. Related somewhat to the 1979 Presidential Address title of Marguerite Clifton's "Turning The Corner."

Changes in the attitudes of the Academy's members are beginning to appear. Based upon a response from 25 of the most recently inducted members and 25 from the Fellow Emeriti ranks, a preliminary description of their thought is possible. Those inducted in the past 5 years — younger and the products of a different social, political, economic, and academic environment from that of earlier members — likewise bring a somewhat different perspective of the Academy's role and functions. They desire to maintain their positions as prominent scholars and researchers throughout their professional careers, positions centered in an area of intensive specialization, one effect of which is a turning inward to personal concerns. They readily admit that the demands of being productive scholars and successful teachers limit the time and desire to assume responsibilities in professional organizations or services, which are often confining and retarding.

It has been said that the spread of scholarly interests and research, although indicative of growth, frequently leads to a loss of communication among the Academy's members and a sense of isolation from others who maintain other interests (Barrow, 1980). It frequently divides the profession — a matter of concern to those who view all physical education as a unity, a nondivisible entity, and who see specialization as detrimental to the totality of physical education.

This response from recent members may provide some insight into their expectations for the Academy, which they say is composed of a prestigious group of persons who are respected and admired. Recent members are proud to have been elected to the Academy. But they feel the Academy has a responsibility to lead, to be more visible both within and outside the profession, and to consolidate its voice so as to create a greater impact upon the total program of physical education. In their view, the Academy fails to convey the meaningfulness of its activities; it fails to capture the interest of the younger members and motivate them to catch the spirit of service. While the Academy is a deliberative, philosophic body and an honorary organization, it should provide greater direction and leadership to the profession.

This view does not imply that those who became members earlier are insensitive to the new influences impinging upon the purposes of the Academy. Conversely, many older members have reinforced the views expressed by the most recent ones.

One must realize that there will be some major changes in the composition of the membership at the end of the next 4-year period. The major shift is likely to be from the Active-Fellow into the Emeriti-Fellow ranks, with approximately 50% of the total Active-Fellow class being occupied by members just described.

It is appropriate to note here the guidance of Clark W. Hetherington in supporting the honorary status of the Academy: "High purpose and character in service in the program of the professional sciences are as important as scientific scholarship and research, and vice versa. Real progress depends upon these two traits becoming a working unity in the motives of the higher class of workers" (Leaf, 1974).

The future agenda for the Academy, then, is basically one of establishing priorities for strengthening its own purposes and its role in the profession, and of establishing a means of arriving at mutually recognized and accepted goals to be pursued to the commencement of the 21st century.

The agenda does not abandon the fundamental purposes of the Academy which have so long endured. The steadfast adherence to the stated purposes and to their spirit has lent distinction and uniqueness to the Academy. This distinction is to be preserved and sharpened lest the Academy assume the commonality of purpose with other existing organizations, who themselves are proceeding cautiously in trying to find themselves and the particular relevance of their functions.

The importance of providing strong support to Academy purposes is underlined by Thomas Watson, Jr. in his analysis of factors responsible for successful organizations:

> I firmly believe that any organization in order to survive and achieve success must have a sound set of beliefs on which it premises all of its policies and actions. Next, I believe that the most important single factor is faithful adherence to those beliefs. And finally, I believe if an organization is to meet the challenges of a changing world, it must be prepared to change everything about itself except those beliefs. In other words, the basic philosophy, spirit and drive of an organization have far more to do with its relative achievements than do technological or economic resources, organizational structure, innovation and timing. All of these things weigh heavily in success. But they are, I think transcended by how strongly the people in the organization believe in its basic precepts and how faithfully they carry them out. (Peters & Waterman, 1982, p. 280)

The agenda for the future would establish an *innovation audit*. Nearly every human endeavor that attempts to be effective and successful devises a process of bringing any new, problem-solving idea into use (Kanter, 1983). Thus, an innovation audit can suggest how to determine member aspirations, improve communications, develop new programs, find new ways to disseminate resolutions, integrate and synthesize isolated interest units, and bring concepts and theoretical relationships into reality.

The innovation audit would be generated from detailed information from interviews with Academy Fellows of Active, Emeriti, Corresponding, and Associate ranks. This task of completing the agenda does not unduly challenge the Academy, whose membership possesses exceptional talent with impressive credentials and probably maintains as much as, if not more, capability than any group in this profession.

The agenda should include an *innovation audit data base*, which would use the basic data yielded by the *structure* indicated in the Academy's by-laws and in the *functions* expressed in its statements of purposes. It would, as well, use sources of information derived from successful systems in other academies similar to this Academy. The data constructed by the Arthur Esslinger study of 1967 could serve as a model.

When interpreted, the data would show how to improve the organizational base for operation, would reflect the aspirations worthy of the Academy's adoption, would show how Academy programs could positively influence the profession, and would suggest possible funding sources to implement innovative, approved proposals.

The suggested future agenda is an alternative to the traditional programs; it allows a penetration of ideas which take their outline and coloration from the minds of all the members. Some important questions to be answered by the innovation audit are: What perceptions of the art and science of human movement and physical activity, and of professional reality, are now emerging that will likely be dominant in the year 2000? Having identified these, what do we, the members, think of them? Which might be solid, promising, and worthy of advancing?

In accepting innovation we need not fear a shift from traditional values. The Academy maintains the freedom to choose its own ideas and the courage to act upon them. But any set of ideas that receives wide acceptance will closely resemble a reality perceived by many of the members. The Academy will be effective only as long as it articulates the values and professional conceptions of its members. When it enunciates ideas or promotes programs that are not realistic as seen by its supporters, it will be rejected; and no amount of extensive mechanical procedures will make its views acceptable.

The Academy can be the wellspring of direction for the profession in a period of environmental and personnel change. We can best contribute by preserving, improving, and strengthening functions within the context of our basic purposes, and in so doing we will positively help to preserve a vital component of human life.

A healthy profession requires productive and innovative organizations capable of changing directions as conditions change. I believe we, the members of the Academy, will direct its future, and that future will be shaped by our own initiative and self-reliance.

"Where your treasure is, there will your heart be also" (Matt. 6:21). It is in the future that the Academy must build its treasure of ideas and spirit. The foundation of these ideas and spirit is always in *giving*, not in *taking*, and not in the pursuit of self-interest.

REFERENCES

ALLEY, L.E. A time for action. *The Academy Papers*, 1978.

BARROW, H.M. The academy—Today and tomorrow. *The Academy Papers*, 1980.

CLIFTON, M.A. Turning the corner. *The Academy Papers*, 1979.

ESSLINGER, A.A. Academies—Their organization and operation. *The Academy Papers*, 1967.

JEWETT, A.E. A new focus? *The Academy Papers*, 1974.

KANTER, R.M. The change masters: Innovation for productivity in the American mode. New York: Simon & Schuster, 1983.

LEAF, C.A. *History of the American Academy of Physical Education, 1950-1970.* Unpublished doctoral dissertation, University of Utah, Salt Lake City, 1974.

METHENY, E. *Movement and meaning.* New York: McGraw-Hill, 1968.

NAISBITT, J. *Megatrends: Ten new directions transforming our lives.* New York: Warner Books, 1982.

PETERS, T.J., & Waterman, R.H. *In search of excellence.* New York: Harper & Row, 1982.

WEISS, R.A. Let's take a position. *The Academy Papers*, 1973.

PRESIDENTS
American Academy of Physical Education

*1926–30	Clark W. Hetherington
*1930–38	Robert Tait McKenzie
*1938–39	Robert Tait McKenzie
	Mabel Lee
*1939–41	John Brown, Jr.
1941–43	Mabel Lee
*1943–45	Arthur H. Steinhaus
*1945–47	Jay B. Nash
*1947–49	Charles H. McCloy
*1949–50	Frederick W. Cozens
*1950–51	Rosalind Cassidy
1951–52	Seward C. Staley
*1952–53	David K. Brace
1953–54	Neils P. Neilson
1954–55	Elmer D. Mitchell
1955–56	Anna S. Espenschade
*1956–57	Harry A. Scott
*1957–58	Charles C. Cowell
*1958–59	Delbert Oberteuffer
1959–60	Helen Manley
1960–61	Thomas E. McDonough, Sr.
1961–62	M. Gladys Scott
1962–63	Fred V. Hein
1963–64	Carl L. Nordly
*1964–65	Eleanor Metheny
1965–66	Leonard A. Larson
*1966–67	Arthur A. Esslinger
1967–68	Margaret G. Fox
1968–69	Laura J. Huelster
1969–70	H. Harrison Clarke
1970–71	Ruth M. Wilson
1971–72	Ben W. Miller
1972–73	Raymond A. Weiss
1973–74	Ann E. Jewett
1974–75	King J. McCristal
*1975–76	Leona Holbrook
1976–77	Marvin H. Eyler
1977–78	Louis E. Alley
1978–79	Marguerite A. Clifton
1979–80	Harold M. Barrow
1980–81	Aileene S. Lockhart
1981–82	Earle F. Zeigler
1982–83	Edward J. Shea (current)
1983–84	Henry J. Montoye (elect)

*Deceased